GUTS:
LEGENDARY BLACK RODEO COWBOY
BILL PICKETT

GUTS

Legendary
Black Rodeo
Cowboy
**BILL
PICKETT**

CECIL JOHNSON

THE SUMMIT GROUP • FORT WORTH, TEXAS

THE SUMMIT GROUP
1227 West Magnolia, Suite 500 • Fort Worth, Texas 76104

95 96 97 98 99   5 4 3 2

Library of Congress Cataloging-in-Publication Data
Johnson, Cecil.
    Guts: legendary black rodeo cowboy Bill Pickett: a biography /
by Cecil Johnson.
    p. cm.
    Includes bibliographical references.
    ISBN 1-56530-162-5: $19.95
    1. Pickett, Bill, ca. 1860-1932. 2. Afro-American cowboys—United
States—Biography. I. Title.
    GV1833.6.P5J64 1994
    791.8—dc20
    [B]   94-38591
                                                       CIP

Cover and book design by David Sims
Cover photograph by Truitt Rogers •Author photograph courtesy of Fort Worth Star-Telegram

3 9510 2003 3558 9

For Linda, Ceiti, and a stalwart friend
and worthy tennis foil, Jeff Guinn.

TABLE OF CONTENTS

FOREWORD

AS A GREAT-GRANDSON OF BILL PICKETT, I AM elated by the growing interest in the life and deeds of my great-grandfather. The recognition he has achieved in recent years is an overdue tribute to a remarkable individual and simultaneously an acknowledgment of the important contributions of African Americans to the heritage of the American West.

My mother died when I was about five years old. So along with my father, Frank Sr., and my sister, Cue Shanklin-Thau, I moved in with my grandmother, Bessie Pickett Phillips, who was the second oldest daughter of Bill Pickett. It did not matter if we were at the breakfast table, sitting on the back porch, or walking through the park, she always talked about her father, Bill Pickett, and other cowboys of Texas and Oklahoma.

As I grew older I went to the movies and saw most of the cowboys she mentioned, but no Bill Pickett and no black cowboys at all, not even in disparaging roles. There was no mention of black cowboys in the *Wild West* magazines or in any of the western novels. I could not understand why.

Bill Pickett performed at rodeos for more than forty years. He rode broncs and bulls and was an all-around professional cowboy, as well as a rodeo champion. He performed in the circus, in world fairs, and Wild West shows. He exhibited his skills in Europe, South America, and Canada, as well as the United States. He lived most of the last twenty-five years of his life on or near the famous 101 Ranch in Oklahoma.

My great-grandfather was born on December 5, 1870, in Travis County, Texas, the second of thirteen children born to Thomas Jefferson Pickett, a former slave, and his wife, Mary (Janie) Virginia Elizabeth Gilbert. After going through the fifth grade, Bill Pickett became a ranch hand, developed his roping and riding skills, and invented a type of steer wrestling known as bulldogging. That involved his riding up alongside a steer, throwing himself on its back, gripping its horns, and twisting its neck until he could sink his teeth into its upper lip or nose, and then throwing his hands wide and throwing himself backwards, his weight and the painful grip of his teeth bringing the animal over on its side.

He got the idea from seeing a cattle dog holding a cow by the nose or upper lip. He developed this technique out of his experiences of working cattle in the Texas brush country, where roping was often impossible, and the cowboy sometimes had to throw an animal by wrapping its tail around his saddle horn or wrestling it to the ground by its horns. Bill Pickett was grappling ineffectually with an unusually stiff-necked longhorn cow when he remembered a big mastiff, which could bring rebellious steers to the ground by gripping their noses in his teeth, the manner of the bulldogs that "baited" English bulls for sport centuries ago. Pickett sank his teeth into the animal's nostrils or lip and immediately brought her down.

When he was only ten, he discovered that he could throw a calf by this method and also hold calves with his teeth during branding. He eventually began to regularly use his bulldogging skills both in catching wild cattle in the brush and in putting on exhibitions. Sometime in the late 1880s my great-grandfather became at least a semiprofessional, appearing at county fairs and similar occasions.

On December 2, 1890, he married Maggie Turner, by whom he had nine children, and the responsibilities of a growing family stimulated greater professionalism. He bulldogged at first in various Texas cow towns and then, sometimes in association with some of his brothers, in other western states, Canada, and Mexico. In 1905, he received national attention (*Leslie's Illustrated Weekly*, August 10, 1905) as "a man who outdoes the fiercest dog in utter brutality."

My great-grandfather stood five feet, seven inches tall and weighed only 145 pounds, but was "hard and tough as whalebone, with . . . powerful shoulders and arms." He wore a small mustache. In 1907, he was signed to a contract with the Miller Brothers' 101 Ranch Wild West Show, with headquarters in Oklahoma's Cherokee Strip. He became one of the principal attractions, its star performer, and under its auspices attained national and international fame, appearing for a decade all over the United States, in Canada, Mexico, Argentina, and England. During this period, the exploit which he had invented was accepted as a regular and leading rodeo event, although it was soon considerably modified.

Few if any of Pickett's imitators were willing, at least not for long, to follow the original technique of "taking a mouthful" of a steer's upper lip or nostrils and, depending on the grip of the teeth and the weight of the body, throw the animal. Some so-called bulldoggers were simply "twisting them down" by hand. Objections by humane societies contributed to the abandonment of the true bulldog style.

For some time he continued at least to simulate his old bulldog stunt, and for publicity purposes he was sometimes fined for "cruelty to animals." But bulldogging for awhile survived vestigially with the bulldogger. Bill Pickett also was credited with such fabulous feats as throwing a buffalo bull and a fully antlered bull elk. Although at various times nearly every bone in his body was cracked or broken, he so thoroughly dominated the animals that no steer or bull ever tried to gore him after being bulldogged.

My great-grandfather's most harrowing experience was undoubtedly in the Mexico City bullring (December 23, 1908), after Joe Miller for publicity purposes had callously bet that Pickett could stay on a Mexican fighting bull for fifteen minutes. During at least five minutes of that time, Pickett would be grappling with the bull unless he succeeded in throwing it sooner. But the Mexican audience, enraged at the insult to their national sport, showered him and his horse with mis-siles, ranging from fruit and cushions to bottles, brickbats, and knives. His horse was badly gored, and Pickett was severely gashed and had three ribs broken. Although he won the bet by staying on the bull's back for seven-and-a-half minutes, he never succeeded in throwing the animal, and he and his horse narrowly escaped with their lives.

My great-grandfather semiretired from rodeo shortly after 1916. He went back to work at the 101 Ranch in 1920, set-tling nearby on a little ranch he had bought near Chandler, Oklahoma. In 1931, when the ranch was in serious financial difficulties, he tried to help out. While roping a stallion on foot in late March of 1932, he tripped and fell and was kicked in the head by the stampeding horse. He died in the Ponca City hospital on April 2, 1932.

Bill Pickett's funeral was one of the largest ever held in the state of Oklahoma. He was buried at White Eagle Monument in Marland, Oklahoma. The Cherokee Strip Cowboy Association erected a limestone marker, and Colonel Zack Miller, who declared that Bill Pickett was "the greatest sweat-and-dirt cowhand that ever lived," wrote a poem in his honor.

My great-grandfather's principal memorial, however, is the rodeo event he created without which, although in a drastical-ly modified form, no rodeo is complete. Homer Croy's verdict is that he "contributed more to rodeos than any other one per-son." Innumerable books and articles about the 101 Ranch and

Wild West Show, rodeo, and the western cattle country give significant attention to this fabulous character.

— FRANK S. PHILLIPS, JR.
Great-grandson of Bill Pickett

Frank S. Phillips, Jr. is a resident of Silver Springs, Maryland, and a systems analyst with the Thurgood Marshall Justice Center. He has two sons, who are attorneys. His father is a former rodeo cowboy.

A C K N O W L E D G M E N T S

I am grateful to Frank S. Phillips, Jr., one of Bill Pickett's great-grandsons, for writing the foreword to this book. As one of the two hundred fifteen living direct descendants of the legendary cowboy in 1994, Phillips has worked tirelessly to keep the memory of his distinguished forebear alive and unsullied. Scores of other descendants of Pickett's brothers, sisters, and cousins are actively involved in that effort, which is highlighted frequently by Pickett family reunions. Their endeavors are performing a valuable service to American history.

MOST OF THE PUBLISHED ATTEMPTS TO CAPSULIZE
the life of Bill Pickett end by citing all or part of the elegiac
poem written in the cowboy's honor by Colonel Zack Miller of
the 101 Ranch. I have chosen instead to begin this book by
citing that poem, which was written shortly after Pickett's
death. Here is the whole poem:

Old Bill is Dead
by Colonel Zack Miller

Old Bill has died and gone away,
Over the "Great Divide."
Gone to a place where the preachers say
Both saint and sinner will abide.
If they "check his brand" like I think they will
It's a running hoss they'll give to Bill.
And some good wild steers till he gets his fill.
With a great big crowd for him a thrill.
Bill's hide was black but his heart was white,

He'd sit up through the coldest night
to help a "doggie" in a dyin' fight
To save a dollar for his boss.
And all Bill wanted was a good fast hoss,
Three square meals and a place to lay
His tired self at the end of day.
There's one other thing, since I've come to think
Bill was always willing to take a drink.
If the job was tough, be it hot or cold,
You could get it done if Bill was told.
He'd fix the fence, or skin a cow,
Or ride a bronc, and EVEN PLOW,
Or do anything, if you told him how.
Like many men in the old-time West,
On any job, he did his best.
He left a blank that's hard to fill
For there never will be another Bill.
Both White and Black will mourn the day
That the "Biggest Boss" took Bill away.

That is a moving tribute to a man and a friend that borders on literature. It is obvious that Miller's feelings for Pickett ran much deeper than those of employer to mere employee. The poem, despite all of its good intent, presents a problem for some modern readers that can't be ignored. That glitch occurs in the line: "Bill's hide was black but his heart was white." Of course, Miller thought he was paying Pickett the highest compliment a

white man could give a black man. He was elevating Pickett to
the status of an honorary white, declaring him an exception to
the run-of-the-mill blacks who were presumed by nature not to
be brave, conscientious, or loyal.

Miller, of course, was absolutely correct in his forecast that
"White and Black will mourn the day | That the 'Biggest Boss'
took Bill away." Whites and blacks who are interested in the
culture of the American West must look back in admiration at
Bill Pickett, a true hero of the American West, whose achievements and character transcended race.

I realize it is anachronistic to criticize Zack Miller for
expressing himself from the mind-set and in the vernacular of
his times. That was the only perspective he could have been
expected to have, and he was trying to be charitable. The line,
however, cannot help but strike the modern reader, white or
black, as patronizing. And that is what is wrong with most of
what has been written about Bill Pickett. It is because of the
condescension and racial stereotyping in most of those
accounts that the name Bill Pickett rings only a small bell in
the minds of most Americans, black and white.

One of the primary sources of information about Pickett,
the source from which many magazine articles have been
derived, is Fred Gibson's *Fabulous Empire*, which is primarily
about Zack Miller and the 101 Ranch. The book, published in
1946, contains invaluable information about Pickett, but it is
laced with so much of the language and imagery of bigotry that
few contemporary Americans, white or black, can stomach

much of it. One has to be doing research for a story or book to command the patience to stick to it.

In his very good book *Bill Pickett Bulldogger*, Colonel Bailey Hanes makes some giant steps toward repairing the damage done to the image of Bill Pickett by Gibson and some of those who have spun yarns off his book. His intentions, like Zack Miller's, are noble. It is noteworthy that Colonel Hanes was among the leaders of the fight that led to Pickett's belated induction into the National Rodeo Cowboy Hall of Fame in Oklahoma City. Nevertheless Colonel Hanes is a good southern gentleman of roughly Zack Miller's generation and his Pickett comes through as something of an Uncle Remus as well.

That, of course, is a substantial improvement over the caricature of a minstrel man that emerges from Gibson's pages. The primary problems for the modern reader with Hanes's book are that it keeps some of those stereotypes, and it digresses excessively to matters only remotely related to Bill Pickett.

My endeavor here is to offer an adaptation of the story of a genuine American hero, a man of courage and dignity, who did some incredible things that all Americans, white, black, and otherwise, should know about. I have tried to make this account truthful, enjoyable, and worthy of Bill Pickett and all the less-celebrated cowboys, black and white, who have contributed so abundantly to the enrichment of America's cultural heritage.

Chapter One

....

Big Bulls in Cowtown

ᴥ

ILL PICKETT HAD ALREADY STAKED HIS CLAIM to stardom when he arrived in Fort Worth in late March 1905. He came to flaunt his stuff for herds of cattle barons, their families, and cowhands making their annual pilgrimage to that North Central Texas cattle and railroad center. During tours from Mexico to Canada, dazzled spectators had transformed Willie B. Pickett of Taylor, Texas, into a phenomenon. He became known as the Dusky Demon, the daredevil Negro who downed and held wild steers with his bulldog strong teeth.

Pickett had, in less than a decade, burned his brand onto a part of cowboy exhibitions and competitions with which he will be forever identified. A hundred years after the first time he performed his magic for public viewing on a full-grown and thoroughly uncooperative longhorned steer, Pickett would be remembered as the inventor of bulldogging (now officially called steer wrestling in rodeo circuits). Others were reported to have thrown steers in public exhibitions, but none of them did it as spectacularly. His technique was called for obvious reasons the "bite 'em style."

The diminutive cowboy rode alongside a steer, vaulted from the saddle from five or six feet away, landed on the head and neck of the animal, grabbed a horn in each hand, and dug his heels in the dirt to slow the beast, which weighed a half-ton or more. With a horn grasped firmly in each hand, the 145-pound cowboy twisted the steer's head until he could reach its upper lip with his mouth. Pickett then sank his strong white teeth into the tender flesh of the steer's upper lip and bore down with all the force of a bulldog.

The intense pain of the bite usually caused the steer to freeze in its tracks. That's when Pickett flung his arms wide in a "Look, no hands" gesture and threw himself backward, bringing the steer down with him.

It was said that, once bitten and thrown, no steer would try to attack Pickett, just as no steer out on the range would charge a bulldog that had brought it down. That just proved, some said, that cattle aren't as dumb as people may think.

While he was unloading his horse from a train at the Fort Worth station, Pickett had no inkling that he was about to have an encounter that would alter the course of his life. He had just come to Cowtown to tussle with the big steers, make a few dollars, visit his cousin and his family, and pick up some piece goods and trinkets to take home to his wife, Maggie, and his daughters.

Colonel Zack Miller, of the famous 101 Ranch in Bliss, Oklahoma, also did not suspect that this meeting with Pickett would begin a friendship that would endure for the next quarter of a century. The Oklahoma cattleman, of course, had not seen Pickett's act before, although he'd heard much about it. Years later he would say of Pickett's specialty that it took "guts, bull strength, and the same peculiar sense of timing that makes art out of dancing."

It was not a mere coincidence that the burly, full-voiced cattle trader was in Fort Worth. Miller was there specifically to see and meet that dusky rascal everybody was talking about. Of course, it really didn't take much of a reason to get Zack Miller to mosey down to Fort Worth, where a man could have a good time regardless of his tastes.

Sparked by the railroads and the packing houses, the population was exploding and all kinds of new businesses and industries were springing up. The result was a town with a split personality.

There was Hell's Half Acre filled with saloons and brothels, gambling and shoot-outs. Despite the efforts of the reformers to civilize the place, there was still enough opportunity for sinning and general mischief to satisfy the needs of any trail-dusty cowboy thirsting for a break in the monotony and new tales to take back to the range.

Then there was the cosmopolitan part of Fort Worth, which made some people call it the "Queen of the Prairie," with its playhouses, concert halls, churches, and social clubs.

Zack Miller could fit into both cow towns. He looked the part of cattle baron from the tip of his peaked, clefted Stetson to the heels of his ornately embossed boots. In between the boots and the hat, Miller's thick-set, six-foot frame was well-fitted in its pin-striped dark blue suit. His wide neck was covered by a high collar, held aloft by a large knotted silver and maroon cravat. Miller's physiognomy was striking. His heavy brows, a mark of the Miller clan, protruded over piercing brown eyes that seemed to bore through the object on which they were focused. His thin lips looked as if he were grinding his teeth, when he was not speaking. He had a commanding air of supreme self-confidence, and he projected the aura of a man's man in a rough world.

Zack Miller . . . looked the part of cattle baron from the tip of his peaked, clefted Stetson to the heels of his ornately embossed boots.

Zack Miller was good at mixing business and pleasure. While enjoying himself, he could usually make a good buy, swap, or sale or two in Fort Worth's big bulls market. He supposed he'd have come even if he wasn't on a mission to seek out Pickett, but his main purpose for being there was the cowboy. His older brother, Colonel Joe Miller had dispatched him to Fort Worth with strict orders to take in Pickett's performance, and, if it lived up to expectations, to talk the so-called Dusky Demon into coming up to the 101. He had seldom seen Joe quite as serious about anything. He was almost as determined about Pickett as he was about "The Great I Am," the name he gave to a boar hog he paid $4,500 for when he got a mind to go into raising hogs. Zack and George Miller had laughed at Joe, when in addition to the Great One he bought forty top Duroc-Jersey gilts at $6,500 apiece to provide the boar companionship.

The phrase "hog heaven" didn't do justice to the accommodations provided for The Great I Am. He munched on scientifically prepared food in an apartment kept cool by oscillating fans, and the high-priced sows were brought in frequently for his entertainment. The Great I Am proved prolific, and in no time there was a passel of gilts of breeding age ripe for the market. Joe advertised his gilts in pig industry, agricultural, and scientific publications. The response was stupendous. Buyers came from hither, thither, and the unheard of to buy one of the brood of The Great I Am. They almost fought each other at the auction, and Joe Miller doubled his investment. Before long the 101 Ranch had more than five thousand registered Duroc-Jersey sows and had become a focal point of the hog industry in the middle of cattle country.

So when Joe Miller was as determined about this Pickett fella, Zack Miller didn't laugh. He'd come to give the Dusky Demon a serious look-see.

Pickett's Dusky Demon moniker had been hung on him by Doug McClure, an aggressive promoter the cowboy hooked up with in 1903. The alliterative tag suggested that Pickett possessed some kind of supernatural powers that enabled him to cast a spell on the steers. The demon characterization also may have served to explain to the spectators the apparent dispropor-tion between Pickett's physical stature and the sizes of the ani-mals he handled with such dexterity. Pickett was a small man, barely five feet, seven inches in height and weighing only 145 pounds. Most of that weight was concentrated in his powerful shoulders and forearms. He had enormous hands for a man his size. He was, in effect, big without being large. Pickett's sunken features and piercing black eyes gave him a brooding aspect, except when he broke into a broad gleaming smile. That hap-pened often, especially after he had taken down a big steer and was bowing to the audience. He fancied bright red shirts and long over-the-calf boots.

Pickett's sunken features and piercing black eyes gave him a brooding aspect, except when he broke into a broad gleaming smile. That happened often . . .

McClure had a talent for using words to cast a spell on potential audiences. In Pickett he spotted a fantastic subject for use in working his promotional magic.

Prior to becoming linked to "Mister Cowboy," as McClure had come to be called because of his success in promoting cow-boy acts, Pickett had been managed by Lee Moore, a rancher for whom he had worked on a large spread near Rockdale, Texas. Moore was a portly man with cold eyes, a ruddy com-plexion, and a shady past. He spotted the showstopping poten-tial of Pickett's derring-do one day when he and the hands were loading some steers into the railroad stock pens for ship-ment to Kansas City.

One of the animals, a big three-year-old longhorn, broke away and headed for the thickets. Pickett took after him on his horse, Chico. The horse raced around to the steer's right side and began maneuvering to force the panicked animal to turn left, back to the stock pens. But before the steer could turn, Pickett jumped from the saddle, put a neck and horn hold on the steer and tumbled it onto its side. He then dug his teeth into the steer's upper lip and raised his arms to show that he had the animal under control.

Moore told Pickett: "That was some stunt," as he and another cowboy rode up and put their ropes on the steer. Pickett did it again a few days later at Hempstead, which convinced the rancher there was gold, figuratively speaking, in Pickett's teeth. He carried Pickett and two of his brothers to county fairs and western sporting events in Houston, San Angelo, Dublin, and Fort Worth. Pickett earned a percentage of the admissions take for putting on his novel exhibitions. When the crowds in Texas reacted the way he expected them to, Moore saw dollar signs across the state lines. The farther out of Texas Pickett traveled, the farther ahead of him word-of-mouth enhanced his reputation.

Milt Hinkle, a cowboy, bulldogger, and promoter himself, described the crowd's reactions to Pickett's actions:

> Every time Pickett busted a steer to the ground, his strong white teeth clamped tight on the critter's lip, the crowd stood up on their hind legs and cheered. It was the trip to Phoenix, Arizona, that put Bill over in a big way, and also in Tucson.

The demonstration that had so impressed Moore was not, however, the first time Pickett had bulldogged a steer. He had been practicing that stunt for years. He began with calves, after watching cow dogs catch steers in the brush country. Pickett gave different versions of how he first jumped into bulldogging. By his own account, Pickett's first takedown of a fully-matured bovine was a cow.

He said he was working on a ranch near Taylor and was told to follow a cow that had hidden a newborn calf in a thicket and bring them both out. Knowing that the cow would steer him in the wrong direction if she knew she was being followed, Pickett headed in the opposite direction until he spotted where the cow was going. When he abruptly turned his horse 180 degrees and sped back toward them. In a panic, the calf jumped up and ran bawling its lungs out. The cow called to the calf, which then came back to its mother's side. By then that was one angry cow.

Pickett wanted to rope the cow, but he couldn't because there wasn't room in the thickets to swing a loop. The best he could do was to throw the rope underhanded at the animal. And that just made the cow madder. In her rage, she charged at the horse and rider with horns lowered with the intent to do some serious hooking. To prevent his horse from being punctured, Pickett reached down and grabbed the cow's horns. The cow recoiled and pulled Pickett off his horse, but he held on to the horns when his feet hit the ground. Picket told Hinkle:

> I just had to keep that old cow from running her horns into my little horse, Chico. That cow scared my horse

so bad he ran off and left me alone with the darned old cow. So I had to bust her to the ground, and I did it by putting my left arm under her horn with my right hand holding her other horn and twisting her old neck until she went down. I was so mad at that old cow for trying to hurt my little Chico, and I tried to pull her eye out with my thumb. I grabbed her by the lips with my teeth and started biting her. I was sure mad at that cow. I took hold of her like old Spike (a catch dog reputed to be the best in Texas at holding a cow). I knew if I let her up that we'd have a fast foot race, and I never was fast on my feet . . .

Finally, Pickett's boss and another cowhand came and roped the cow. They did not, however, bring Pickett's horse with them. So he had to walk back to the herd.

It was at this time, while walking back to the herd that I conceived the idea of jumping from my horse to the cattle's head and horns, catching them with my teeth and holding them like the bulldogs did, as it would not cut up the stock as much as the dogs did.

That version really does not conflict with reports that he had been biting down cattle since he was a boy. Previously, however, he had not been leaping from a horse to do it.

By the time Pickett got to Phoenix, he had already parted company with Moore and had linked up with McClure (Mister Cowboy). The separation from Moore was partly about Pickett's feeling that he wasn't getting enough of the admissions money. But also it had to do with McClure's guaranteeing bigger audiences. McClure had a gift for gab as long as the Red River. He was a master hustler and an expert on crowd psychology.

Pickett, at the time, was known as Will Pickett. McClure added the "Dusky Demon" for the sensational effect. However, in addition to conjuring up notions of some kind of black-magic powers possessed by the black cowboy, there was a very mundane reason for the nickname. Many prejudiced cowboys did not cotton to the idea of competing against or being on the same program with a black man, and in some places participation in such events by blacks was officially or unofficially banned.

> *Many prejudiced cowboys did not cotton to the idea of competing against or being on the same program with a black man, and in some places participation in such events by blacks was officially or unofficially banned.*

The Dusky Demon alias allowed McClure to advertise Pickett's act without spelling out that he was black. When the crowds found out, in most cases, it didn't matter because they were so taken with the act. In most places, however, the subterfuge was unnecessary, for as the word of Pickett's derring-do spread, people wanted to see his act for themselves. When Pickett arrived in Cheyenne, Wyoming, in 1904 for that bustling cattle town's Frontier Days celebration, there were twenty thousand people eagerly awaiting his appearance.

Newspapers had featured stories of how the "Negro from Taylor, Texas" could single-handedly, "unaided by any rope or contrivance," bring down a wild bucking steer with his teeth.

Pickett lived up to his billing, and the Cheyenne crowds cheered him wildly. At one performance the applause was so infectious that, after throwing a steer that had given him a particularly rough time and releasing it, Pickett ran and caught the animal and busted it down again. In an article in the October 8, 1904, edition of *Harper's Weekly* headlined "Cowboy Festival in Wyoming," J. D. Howe described that memorable man-versus-beast encounter:

> With the aid of a helper, Pickett chased the steer until he was in front of the grandstand. Then he jumped from the saddle and landed on the back of the animal, grasped its horns, and brought it to a stop within a dozen feet. By a remarkable display of strength, he twisted the steer's head until its nose pointed straight into the air, the animal bellowing with pain and its tongue protruding in its effort to secure air. Again and again the Negro was jerked from his feet and tossed in the air, but his grip on the horns never once loosened, and the steer failed in its efforts to gore him.
>
> Cowboys with lariats rushed to Pickett's assistance, but the action of the combat was too rapid for them. Before help could be given, Pickett, who had forced the steer's nose into the mud and shut off its wind, slipped, and was tossed aside like a piece of paper. There was a scattering of cowboys as he jumped to his feet and ran for his horse. Taking the saddle without touching the stirrup, he ran the steer to a point opposite the judges stand, again jumped on its back, and threw it. Twice was the Negro lifted from his feet, but he held on with the tenacity of a bulldog. Suddenly Pickett dropped the steer's head and grasped the upper lip of the animal

with his teeth, threw his arms wide apart to show he
was not using his hands, and sank slowly upon his back.
The steer lost its footing and rolled upon its back, completely covering the Negro's body with its own. The
crowd was speechless with horror, many believing that
the Negro had been crushed: but a second later the
steer rolled to its other side, and Pickett arose unin-
jured, bowing and smiling. So great was the applause
that he again attacked the steer, which had staggered to
its feet, and again threw it after a desperate struggle.

Sensational reports of such hair-raising encounters between
Pickett and half-wild longhorns had fired up both George and
Zack Millers's imaginations to the point where they craved
verification. Joe had seen Pickett's performance in St. Louis.
Yet the other brothers, while trusting their older brother's
judgment, had a deep-seated skepticisim toward both newspaper stories and cowboy word of mouth. Both were susceptible
to exaggeration. A cowboy who couldn't magnify a story until
it sounded ten times better than it actually was couldn't be
trusted with the truth. But if this so-called Dusky Demon was
all they said he was, well, he was an attraction they needed for
the big show the 101 Ranch was going to put on for the
National Editorial Association, which was going to hold its big
annual convention in Guthrie.

George Miller had gotten roped into doing that when he
went to the last editors' convention in St. Louis with Frank
Greer, editor of the *Guthrie Leader*. Greer wanted badly to land
the 1905 convention for Guthrie, but he poor-mouthed

Guthrie's chances of landing it. After all Guthrie, Oklahoma, was "way out in the country" and had nothing in the way of entertainment to offer the editors. Greer was baiting Miller. He knew Miller was proud of Guthrie and he wouldn't allow the jab to go unanswered.

Miller was a tall, rangy, long-faced man with a thick mustache that completely covered his upper lip. In a loud raspy voice, he vowed that the 101 could put on a Wild West show "with a hundred cowboys that would push those editors' eyes right out of their sockets." Greer proffered that promise of a full day of eye-popping entertainment at the most fantastic working cattle ranch in the world to the corralled editors, and Joe tied up the sale with a colorful tour de force on the scenery, buffalo, Indians, cattle, and the exciting riding, roping, and shooting they'd be privileged to witness. Besides, he pointed out, it would be so different from all their previous conventions in cities. They'd experience something new, life out on the frontier, up close and personal. They'd get real manure on their shoes.

The editors were wild about the idea of going to the Wild West and roughing it. It was something most of them had dreamed about as boys. It was a chance of a lifetime. What did it matter if the hotel accommodations wouldn't be up to snuff. The convention would be the stuff they would tell their grandchildren about. The cry went up: "See you in Guthrie next year! On to Guthrie in 1905! Go West, Mr. Editor!"

Finding that crucial ingredient to assure that the editors were not disappointed was why Zack Miller had scooted down to Fort Worth to see if this Pickett character was for real. After watching Pickett subdue two of the orneriest hoofed mammals he'd ever seen, Zack Miller was convinced that Pickett was not only right for the show, but also that his act was the most exciting thing he'd ever seen done in any kind of western arena. When Pickett bit into that first big black-and-white bull's snout, fell back with his arms spread apart, and then brought the bellowing, slobbering, kicking beast to the ground beside him, Miller almost fell out of his seat. He choked on a big swallow of cigar juice.

Will Rogers introduced Pickett to Zack Miller. Rogers had urged him to make the Fort Worth show when Pickett passed through Fort Worth on his way to his family's home in Taylor, where he planned to rest and recuperate. Pickett had been in the Zack Mulhall show with Rogers at the St. Louis World's Fair. The drawling, straw-haired wiseacre had said simply, "Bill, I'd like you to meet Colonel Zack Miller of the 101 Ranch," and just stood grinning his wide grin and toying with a rope. Pickett and Miller shook hands, and Pickett acknowledged that he had met Colonel Joe Miller. Zack Miller didn't beat around the bush. He came right out with it. The Editorial Association Convention show just had to have him. He wouldn't take a negative answer. It would be the biggest audience he'd ever performed for, and the money would be well worth his while.

When Pickett shook hands on the deal, he had a feeling in his guts that he was really signing on for more than a short hitch.

There was a huge crowd at Haines Park on the banks of Marine Creek that day. Much of the crowd had been drawn by a newspaper story about a woman roper who was going to rope a running steer from a moving automobile. It was supposed to be the most daring stunt seen in Fort Worth in many years. Something about the changing era's symbolism of the event aroused people's curiosity.

They couldn't get the steer to run in a straight line, and the car's driver couldn't maneuver well enough to get close for an accurate rope toss. After several tries the car stalled. Everyone cheered the effort, but it was interspersed with considerable laughter and a few shouts of, "Get a horse!"

Pickett bulldogged two tough steers during that visit to Fort Worth. *The Fort Worth Telegram* reported his feats, but placed more emphasis on that of another performer. There was no mention of the much ballyhooed roping from the car. The article was headlined simply, "Roping Contest Well-Attended." The reporter wrote:

> Roping and riding exhibitions drew a large crowd of cattlemen and a number of townspeople to Haines Park Tuesday afternoon.
> The feature of the afternoon was an exhibition of fancy roping by Will Rogers. He handled the riata in a most marvelous manner and did stunts with the rope which have never been equaled in this city before. Besides the fancy twisting of the rope, jumping through the loop, etc., he did some excellent work in roping a horse and rider as he rode past.

Miss Annie Shaffer, the girl rider, received great applause when she rode a wild steer, the animal pitching harder than any of the horses.

Will Pickett, who is known as the human bulldog, gave his exhibition of throwing steers with his teeth, riding up to the steer on horseback, then slipping from his horse and grabbing the steers (sic) by the horns.

It would be three years before Pickett would be the subject of the lead story on the front page of that newspaper.

Chapter Two

....

Mayhem in Manhattan

Ⓣ

HIS IS KNOWN: IT DID HAPPEN IN NEW YORK CITY.
Almost everyone who has said or written anything about
Bill Pickett has indicated as much. However, exactly
when and with whom Bill Pickett first went to Madison
Square Garden and bulldogged a runaway steer in the grandstand is one of those occurrences in his extraordinary life that
may be forever shrouded in confusion. The story continues to
be told, but the version depends on who's telling the story and
which one he likes or best suits his purposes.

Sometime in either 1905 or 1914, Pickett bulldogged a
runaway steer in Madison Square Garden. The more important question is whether or not Will Rogers assisted him in
apprehending the runaway beast. If Rogers was there then it
must have occurred in 1905, months before the National
Editorial Association's Convention show in Oklahoma.
Pickett also would have had to have been appearing with

Colonel Zack Mulhall's Wild West Show, as were Rogers and Zack Miller.

The fuzziness about this episode occurred because of two different versions: the Zack Miller rendition, and that of the Mulhall, Will Rogers, and the *New York Herald* version. As Zack Miller recalled it in Fred Gibson's *Fabulous Empire*, published in 1946, Pickett and Rogers were at the center of the action, with Pickett playing the more heroic role and Will Rogers functioning as his rope-twirling backup. The other version features Will Rogers and Lucille Mulhall. Bill Pickett isn't even mentioned. There is no indication that he was even there at the time. It is hard to believe, however, that Colonel Mulhall would have taken his show to New York without Pickett, after the bulldogger's act proved so popular a part of his show at the St. Louis World's Fair in 1904.

The "Rogers as hero" version has a steer getting away from Lucille Mulhall during her roping act and Rogers riding into the grandstand and lassoing it.

That story was ballyhooed in a column in the *New York Herald* that appeared to have been written well after the fact. Moreover, that column appeared to have been based on a re-creation of the facts by either Rogers or Colonel Mulhall or a steering committee. In any event, Rogers used the publicity to catapult himself into vaudeville. Rogers's appearance in New York in 1905 was a pivotal moment in his career, and whatever happened with the runaway steer had much to do with giving him that boost.

Florenz Ziegfield's attention was attracted by the following column:

A Texas steer running among the spectators at the Horse Fair in Madison Square Garden yesterday afternoon caused great excitement for five minutes. That no one was hurt was due to the skill of the cowboy who roped it and guided it back into the arena.

The steer came from Colonel Mulhall's Oklahoma ranch, a dun-colored animal, weighing eight hundred pounds with horns that spread five feet. It is a restive beast and resents its part in the roping exhibition given by Miss Lucille, the Colonel's daughter.

Yesterday the brute had been admitted from the pen at the corner of Fourth Avenue and 26th Street and was urged to its highest speed by six shouting cowboys. It ran to the center of the ring and down toward the entrance at Madison Avenue. As Miss Mulhall followed at top speed and the cowboys drew off, the steer leaped the bars protecting the steps on the 26th Street side.

There was a wild scamper of spectators to get out of its path, but it kept going up the stairs without a misstep. At the top of the first flight, an usher, Claude Lanigan, seized its horns and was thrown across several tiers of seats. Lanigan scrambled to his feet and grabbed the animal's tail just as a number of lassos ensnared him and several chairs.

The steer went up the second and third flights into the balcony and disappeared in the corridor back of the Madison Avenue boxes.

The six cowboys, lariats in hand, were following. The Indian Will Rogers ran up the 27th Street side and headed the steer off. As it passed from the corridor again in view of the spectators, he roped the steer's horns. Alone and afoot, he was no match for the brute's strength, but he swerved it down the steps on the 27th Street side, where it jumped again into the ring. Immediately the ropes of a dozen cowpunchers fell over it from all sides, and with a quick turn it was brought down and led from the track...

The Zack Miller version is undocumented, and he is vague about how he and his cowboys happened to be in New York at the time. But he was definitely there. So was Tom Mix. And according to Miller, so was Bill Pickett. Again, if they were there, it had to be in connection with the Zack Mulhall show. Miller spins such a good yarn about his and his cowboys' exploits in New York in 1905 that it's hard to believe that it is a total fabrication. The part about Bill Pickett and the runaway steer is particularly captivating. Here is how Miller described that action:

> Bill Pickett had his horse backed up on one side of the chute, fixing to do his bulldogging act. Will Rogers was on the other side; he was to do Pickett's hazing. Inside the chute was a big old cactus boomer steer with the map of Texas written all over him.
>
> Bill Pickett quieted down the horse he rode and gave the chute man the nod. The gates jerked apart, and out into the arena lunged Bill's steer.
>
> Best anybody could tell, there was just one thing on that old steer's mind when he quit the chute. That was to head back to the Lone Star State. If he had to climb out over the grandstand, that was all right, too—he'd likely climbed steeper ridges in his time. That old steer

had him a big bellyful of New York's bright lights; he was gone to Texas!

He had the jump on Bill Pickett's horse from the time he quit the chute. He set a straight course across the arena and held it, running like a scared wolf. Bill Pickett's horse wasn't able to catch him.

They tore across the arena, fogging the dust. The steer came to the arena gate and never checked . . . It looked like that old longhorn just sprouted wings and flew. His hind feet knocked the top boards off the high gate, but that didn't slow him. Before him was an aisle of steps leading up onto the first balcony of the grandstand, a trail that was a lot more open than the senderos he was used to following through the huisache thickets along the Nueces River. He took out up it, making four steps at a jump, wringing his tail and roaring as he went.

"It looked like that old longhorn just sprouted wings and flew.'

But he hadn't made his getaway yet. Right behind him, Bill jumped his horse through the hole in the gate and was feeding the spurs to him up that row of steps. Bill had set out to bulldog that steer for the crowd and he aimed to do it if that old Ladino climbed to the moon first.

And popping the boards right on the heels of Bill Pickett's horse rode Will Rogers. Will was a little far behind for good hazing, but he wasn't one to quit a man in a tight. He'd reached down his catch-rope and was shaking out a loop. The crowd was on its feet now, screaming and falling away from both sides of that wild uphill chase. The climbing steer blared like a trumpet. And down at the arena, the announcer, fearing a human stampede, lied like a dirty dog.

"Keep your seats, folks!" he bawled at the top of his voice. "Keep your seats! Don't get panicky! There's not the slightest danger!"

They caught the runaway steer on the third balcony of the grandstand. Will Rogers crowded his scrambling horse up beside Bill Pickett's, reached down, and picked up the steer's heels with his loop. At the same instant Pickett quit his saddle, piling off onto the steer's head.

The crowd watched Bill Pickett hang on to that steer's horns while Will Rogers dragged him, bumping and scrambling and bawling, down out of the stands into the arena where he belonged.

Miller had a rich imagination, but it is hard to believe he made all that up. It is quite possible that the passage of years caused him to get places, times, and people scrambled. In his *Bill Pickett Bulldogger*, Colonel Bailey Hanes relates a remarkably similar episode in 1914, when Pickett appeared at Madison Square Garden and the newspapers hailed him as "The Famous Negro Cowboy Bill Pickett." The details are remarkably similar, but the role of Will Rogers is played by a cowboy named Billy Binder.

Perhaps it happened twice, in which case the Millers, in the latter instance, might be suspected of having caused the steer to bolt in order to create a sensation similar to that of 1905 and attract bigger audiences. Run-amok steers, however, were not an uncommon occurrence in the Wild West shows, and it is not inconceivable longhorn lightning struck twice in Madison Square Garden without any orchestration.

To believe the Zack Miller version, however, is to suggest that a national icon, Will Rogers, was complicit in distorting the truth in order to further his own ambitions. Doing that could be easily rationalized, at that time. Will Rogers could make far better use of the publicity than could Pickett, who at the time was far more renowned than Rogers. The newspapers, however, were not eager to write heroic idylls about Negroes, and Pickett had no aspirations for a vaudeville career. Moreover the story was of more use to Rogers with Lucille Mulhall in it than Pickett.

Run amok steers, however, were not an uncommon occurrence in the wild west shows, . . .

It is noteworthy that, despite their long association, Rogers and Lucille Mulhall had very little to say about Pickett in public or in print—although both were frequent visitors to Pickett's home. In Hanes words: "When Lucille Mulhall visited the 101 Ranch, she also dropped in on Bill and his family. 'Bill is a square shooter,' she once said of him, also contending that he had saved her life on many occasions and was the perfect pickup man in riding events at rodeos and Wild West shows."

Most of Rogers's biographers don't even mention Pickett. Neither does Lucille Mulhall's biographer, Katherine Stansbury; although the famous cowgirl worked with Pickett many times. A cutline to a picture in Reba Collins's *Will Rogers, Courtship and Correspondence* shows Pickett with the Mulhall cast at the St. Louis World's Fair in 1904.

The troubling thing about the Zack Miller version is that he identifies the man who persuaded him to bring his performers to New York only by one name, Gue, which sounds like a pseudonym. Foghorn Clancy, the famous rodeo announcer, however, in his book *My Fifty Years in Rodeo* gives that Gue person the initials G. L., which suggests that he may have been real. This Gue person supposedly was having trouble attracting an audience for his traditional horse show and needed something different for audience appeal. Perhaps Miller simply didn't want to acknowledge that he was just there with the Mulhalls. Perhaps he also felt that he was revealing something that had been kept hidden for more than a quarter of a century, the truth about a heroic incident that had been revised to leave Bill Pickett out of the story.

Almost everyone believes the Zack Miller version, and it has appeared in numerous magazine articles because it is the more exciting story.

It really doesn't matter much. Almost everyone believes the Zack Miller version, and it has appeared in numerous magazine articles because it is the more exciting story. Both versions have come down through the years without anyone being overly concerned that they appear to contradict each other. That is not uncommon in reconstructions from memory of the lives of real people from the days of Wild West shows. Miller's version was picked up and passed on by several writers of western lore, who presumably were aware of the Rogers and Mulhall column. They were convinced that Pickett did tackle a runaway steer in Madison Square Garden at one time or another, and Zack Miller's account sounded too typically Bill Pickett to be untrue.

Chapter Three

Where the Buffalo Roamed

ILL PICKETT HAD SEEN AND WORKED ON SOME of the biggest ranches in Texas during twenty of his thirty-six years on earth. None of them prepared the veteran cowhand and showman for the panorama of the 101 Ranch. Located on the Salt Fork of the Arkansas River in the Cherokee Strip, the 101's undulating terrain stretched for miles in all directions. But it wasn't just the size of the ranch that amazed Pickett. When the Miller brothers and some of the cowhands gave him the grand tour, he was equally impressed by the variety of enterprises in which the Millers were involved. In addition to cattle, they were raising hogs and chickens and growing corn, wheat, and cotton. The ranch was so immense and its workers so absorbed in accomplishing so many different projects that it was like a small country, capable of surviving on its own. There was a butcher shop whose workers delivered meat and milk for miles around, a tannery, a store, and a cafe for employees.

It was the summer of 1905 and the ranch already was so enormous that it took two hundred fifty people to run it and one hundred horses to work the ranges. Someone said it took in close to a half-million dollars a year before expenses.

Pickett couldn't visualize that much money. What he liked was the look of the land, the dark rich earth that produced the sweet blue-stemmed grass on which thousands of head of cattle fattened for the northern markets. Riding along one could scare out wild turkeys, white-tailed deer, and other game. The rambling buffaloes shuffling over the hills and through the valleys provided a vision of serenity that already was vanishing from much of the West.

But it wasn't just the size of the ranch that amazed Pickett . . . he was equally impressed by the variety of enterprises in which the Millers were involved.

The talkative colonels told Pickett the story of how the ranch began under their father, Colonel George Washington Miller, and grew into an empire. The "colonels" were honorary prefixes to the Millers' names. None of them attained that military rank.

Joe Miller was only two years old in 1870 when his father, Colonel George Washington Miller, packed him, his mother, Molly, and all their belongings and left Crab Orchard, Kentucky, to pursue his dream of establishing a new plantation in the West. With some of the money from the sale of his Kentucky cattle and farming holdings, G. W. Miller set himself up in the ranching business in Newtonia, Missouri. He brought his first herd up from Texas to the

Kansas railheads in 1871, when Bill Pickett was only a year old. Miller began accumulating his fortune by trailing herds of sinewy longhorn cattle up from Texas. There they grew like wildflowers, fattening quickly on the rich grasses of the Cherokee land, which he had leased from the Indians. They went from the abundant fields to the Kansas railheads. To be closer to the railheads, Miller soon moved his headquarters to Boxler Springs, Kansas.

For fifteen years, G. W. Miller had a honey of a deal and was well on his way to building the cattle kingdom of his dreams. However, problems developed when some of the other cattlemen started cheating the Indians. Some refused to pay and used guns to get grass and water. The cattlemen also fought among themselves, and men were killed. G. W. Miller and his men held their own with the gunslingers, but they could not push back the waves of farmers who started invading the territory in the 1890s. The farmers wanted the rich, fertile lands of the Cherokee Strip to raise cotton, wheat, and corn, and their voices were heard in Washington, D. C.

Government negotiators asked the Cherokees to cede their claims in the Strip for $1.25 per acre. The Cherokees respectfully declined. After all, their leases to the cattlemen were bringing in close to a quarter-million dollars a year, and they were using the money for schools and other tribal needs. Besides, if they wanted to sell, which they didn't, they could get better deals from the cattlemen, some of whom had already offered three dollars an acre. The Cherokees thought the cattlemen's interest in buying their claim was their ace in the hole. But the government had a bigger trump. Washington exercised its authority to deny the Cherokees permission to sell their claims.

Being part Cherokee on his mother's side, Bill Pickett was intensely interested in how all that wrangling worked out. Joe Miller thought that he might be boring the bulldogger with his long-winded narrative about his family history, but Pickett assured him that he wanted to hear more. Joe Miller went on to tell about the federal government sending three commissioners, the so-called Cherokee Commission, to talk the Cherokees into selling out on government terms. When the Cherokees refused to negotiate, the commissioners simply invalidated the Indians' claims on the grounds that they had never used the land themselves.

The commission also accused the cattlemen of being behind the Cherokees' stubbornness. Therefore, a presidential proclamation was issued in February 1890, directing all cattlemen to remove their herds from the strip in nine months.

Forced to negotiate, the Cherokees agreed to sell out to the government for $1.40 an acre. On August 19, 1893, President Grover Cleveland proclaimed the strip open to white settlement as of noon on September 16. The farmers had won. Most of the cattlemen suffered tremendous losses. Not George Washington Miller.

Zack Miller picked up the story and told how his father had benefited from a favor he had done sixteen years earlier.

After the Poncas were driven from their ancestral homelands in Nebraska, G. W. Miller had helped get Chief White Eagle of the Ponca tribe and his people settled in the strip. The Cherokees, Zack Miller explained, held title to the strip, but they could not refuse to sell land to other tribes. The government could, in fact, relocate any tribes there. Some of the lands of tribes the government had relocated in the strip, however, were made available to whites when the strip was opened to white settlement. The Poncas, however, were allowed to keep the lands G. W. Miller helped them acquire.

In gratitude for G. W. Miller's past favor, White Eagle persuaded the Indian agent on the Ponca reservation to lease Miller one hundred thousand acres for one cent an acre and to allow Miller to continue to lease that land from year to year for as long as he wished. Miller's foothold in the strip was secured, and for the next ten years he set about consolidating and enhancing his realm.

On his deathbed in 1903, G. W. Miller urged his sons Joe, Zack, and George to stay together, keep the leases, and make the 101 bigger and better. From what Pickett could see, the Miller brothers had fulfilled their father's wish, and then some.

G. W. Miller never got to live in the big house he intended to build in the West. He caught pneumonia as a result of walking home to the ranch from the train station in Bliss (now Marland). The big house was completed under the supervision of his widow, Molly, eight months after the colonel was buried next to his father in Crab Orchard Springs, Kentucky. Molly and their daughter Alma moved from Kansas to the strip to live in the big house. Molly Miller took the $30,000 insurance money left to her and bought six one-square-mile sections of land from the Poncas, the first land the Millers actually owned in the strip. Alma Miller married and sold her interests to her brothers. Molly Miller lived in the mansion and served as grande dame of the empire.

Impressed as he was by the Millers' hospitality, the grandeur of the ranch, and the fascinating history the Millers had revealed to him, Pickett could not have imagined that summer that he was forging a connection with that legendary kingdom that would endure for the rest of his life. From 1905 on, Pickett's fate and the fate of the 101 Ranch would become as intertwined as the strands of a hemp lariat.

. . . Pickett could not have imagined that summer that he was forging a connection with that legendary kingdom that would endure for the rest of his life.

As the elaborate preparations for the editor's big show progressed, it dawned on Pickett that this could be the biggest, most spectacular show he'd ever been a part of—bigger in its own way that the St. Louis World's Fair, bigger than the Cheyenne Frontier Days—and he had to be at his best. After all, he was in some select company. The Millers had recruited the best cowboy talent they could find from wherever they could find it. There had been a tremendous nationwide publicity buildup for the event, which was only to be expected for a convention of editors.

Still no one could have predicted the tens of thousands of people who made the pilgrimage to the 101 Ranch to take in the spectacular. Estimates of the crowd ran as high as sixty-five thousand. To haul the hordes, thirty-five special trains were engaged. But they were not sufficient for the job. Even with passengers riding on top of the cars, they were not enough to handle all the traffic between Guthrie and Bliss. Scores of the would-be spectators never got any closer to the 101 than Guthrie. Hustlers rigged up jitney cabs for the trip from Bliss out to the ranch, charging as much as three dollars per passenger. Caravans of people on foot, on horseback, in buggies, and in cars lined the roads to the Salt Fork.

Like an army bivouacking to prepare for a great battle, they came to the shores of the Salt Fork. And it was an army with a gargantuan thirst, because it drained two seep springs dry and guzzled down three boxcar loads of soda water.

The Millers got a break on the cost of security for the event. It didn't cost them anything except the food and drinks consumed by three companies of Oklahoma militia. The militiamen had been ordered there because the word had gotten around that a whole herd of buffalo would be slaughtered and barbecued for the visitors. The humane societies raised such a stink that President Theodore Roosevelt wired the governor of Oklahoma to dispatch the militia to protect the buffalo.

Actually, only one buffalo was to be slaughtered and barbecued for the editors. Instead of explaining that to the governor, Joe Miller let the militia come, and he used them to control the crowd.

Everything was set for the 101 to show its stuff on June 11, 1905. The riders and ropers were ready; the Indians were ready to dance; Geronimo was ready to shoot his last buffalo; and Bill Pickett was ready to bust down the biggest and baddest steer on the place. The day had started bright and sunny, but just before the big show was to begin clouds appeared—a herd of thick black ones rumbling across the sky to the northeast, dragging with them torrents of rain and swirling winds.

Pickett worried that the show would be rained out and he'd miss his big chance to strut his stuff before his biggest audience ever. Joe Miller, however, was even more worried than Pickett. He could see himself having to refund all the admission receipts, and fearing all the good publicity the 101, Guthrie, and Oklahoma had received would be transformed into torrents of vilification and ridicule. The black clouds were definitely headed in their direction. Before long, Miller feared, all those people would be drenched and up to their knees in mud. All those fancy hats and bonnets would be scattered on the soggy landscape for miles in all directions by the howling winds.

A Ponca medicine man named Sits-on-a-Hill appeared to confirm Miller's worst fears.

"Big blow. Big rain. No show," said Sits-on-a-Hill. Lost in his apprehension, Miller did not answer. Then Sits-on-a-Hill told Miller he'd save the show for five head of cattle. Miller, of course, didn't believe Sits-on-a-Hill could do a thing about the approaching storm, but he agreed to pay the price if the medicine man could deliver.

The clouds were coming closer and closer, and the crowd was growing tense and nervous. A hush fell over the encampment as the crowd gazed at the ominous roiling mass of clouds, winds, and rain. Then Sits-on-a-Hill pierced the thick silence with a bloodcurdling shriek and began pounding on a tom-tom. The medicine man had proceeded to a short mesa to perform his rain-stopping ritual. He pounded and crooned, pounded and moaned, pranced and sang, but the clouds kept coming. Then he took a shell out of his pouch and shook it in the direction of the approaching clouds. Simultaneously, he let loose a fierce demonic scream that ricocheted across the landscape like a bolt of lightning. It was a cry of belligerence, as though he were literally commanding the clouds to go away.

. . . the crowd gazed at the ominous roiling mass of clouds, winds and rain. Then Sits-on-a-Hill pierced the thick silence with a blood-curdling shriek and began pounding on a tom-tom. . . .He pounded and crooned, pounded and moaned, pranced and sang, but the clouds kept coming.

And that's what they did. Just as the storm system reached the banks of the Salt Fork it turned abruptly and proceeded eastward along the riverbank. The show could go on. The sun came out bright and blistering. Sits-on-a-Hill's rain-stopping performance, of course, was a tough act to follow. The easterners had heard of Indians dancing to coax rain from the clouds in time of drought, but nothing in their "Wild West dreams" had prepared them for an Indian who could actually make a storm go away by beating on a drum and chanting a lot of incomprehensible mishmash. The folks back home would never believe what they had seen with their own eyes.

With the return of the sun the mile-long parade commenced about 1:30 P.M. It moved east to west, past the grandstand with the Miller brothers leading the way. They looked like the Three Musketeers of the Cherokee Strip with their peaked wide-brimmed hats, sitting astride splendid horses in ornately bejeweled and silver-studded saddles. The National Guard Cavalry was next. Then came Geronimo and three other chiefs in a 1905 Locomobile. More Indians followed and then a parade of cowboys that included Pickett; Tom Mix, who was to go on to become one of Hollywood's biggest cowboy stars; and Milt Hinkle, who would distinguish himself as an all-around cowboy, promoter, and writer.

The show got off to a rousing start with a full-feathered Indian buffalo hunt that was climaxed with Geronimo's buffalo kill. Unfortunately, the aged warrior's aim was bad and he only wounded the animal. (A cowhand had to finish the job.) Geronimo hunted the buffalo from a car that had been loaned for the occasion by a Chicago doctor. Perhaps that's why he hit the buffalo too high in the neck. As promised, Geronimo's kill was butchered, barbecued, and served to the editors.

Bill Pickett's turn came after the bronc riding, the Indian stickball game, and the famous cowgirl Lucille

Mulhall's sensational riding act; and was followed by a staged Indian attack on a wagon train. The enactment was so realistic that most of the spectators thought it was the real thing. Some people in the crowd panicked and were not completely reassured until the grand finale.

That performance was rendered all the more dramatic by being unannounced. Around sundown, ten covered wagons lumbered on the scene heading east, giving the impression of being late for the big spectacular. They unhitched their teams and pitched camp about a quarter of a mile from the grandstand area. The newcomers had hardly settled in, when a swarm of painted Indians riding hell-bent for leather, whooping and screaming like maniacs, arrived. They quickly encircled the newcomers, firing wildly, piling off their horses, swinging tomahawks and shooting people at point-blank range. It looked like a gruesome slaughter. Wagons began bursting into flames. The mules broke loose and stampeded toward the crowd. Just before general panic set in, the Indians jumped on their horses and sped away. Six hundred cowboys and friendly Indians were riding over the hill to the rescue. The rescuers were the grand finale.

Notwithstanding the high drama of the faked attack on the wagon train, Bill Pickett's act was the highlight of the show. After Guy Weadick, promoter, outstanding cowboy, and traveling companion of Pickett's, announced in his circus ringmaster manner that the "Dusky Demon Bill Pickett will throw a steer with his bare hands and teeth." Nine hundred fifty pounds of riled-up longhorn came flying across the area in front of the grandstand with Pickett coming up hard behind it. Pickett caught up with the steer and barreled out of the saddle onto the steer's broad back. He clamped a hand on each horn and dug his heels into the ground to slow the galloping bull. The bull bellowed like a tuba when Pickett twisted its head up and around and dug his incisors firmly into the upper lip. With his bulldog vice grip firmly secured, Pickett flung his arms wide in his trademark gesture of triumph and did a backward dive. The steer plopped over on its side and lay there, kicking its back feet. Pickett bit hard, and the animal ceased all movement.

. . . the crowd was on its feet going wild, clapping and yelling. No other act drew such a reverberating reaction.

Meanwhile the crowd was on its feet going wild, clapping and yelling. No other act drew such a reverberating reaction.

The next day Joe Miller congratulated Pickett on his sensational performance. George Miller, the middle brother, was thin and angular with deep-set, close-together eyes and a weak chin. He was the brother with the best head for business. He looked and dressed the part of the financier, and he was all business. He was not a man given to waste words. Still, he called Pickett's performance "absolutely splendid" and for emphasis shook the cowboy's hand. Joe Miller asked Pickett if he would consider being a part of a traveling 101 show, if they put one together. Pickett told him he would, and then he asked Miller if he paid Sits-on-a-Hill his five head of cattle.

Miller said he had because he'd given his word. But Miller said he knew the medicine man had flimflammed him.

Pickett chuckled because he knew it too. Sits-on-a-Hill had told him: "Big wind, big rain, never cross big river. Most time turn, follow river."

Chapter Four

The Show Must Go On

H AVING DECIDED TO PLUNGE WHOLE HOG INTO
the Wild West show business, the Miller brothers invited Bill Pickett to be a part of their 1907 touring show,
whose highlight would be the Jamestown Exhibition.
When he got the letter, Pickett wasted no time in getting to
the 101 Ranch.

During the previous year, Pickett had been on the rodeo
circuit, performing throughout the western part of the United
States from Texas to California and down into Mexico. He saw
firsthand the devastation in the San Francisco area—the result
of the earthquake and fire that had hit only a few days before
he arrived. When Pickett reached the city, wreaths of smoke
were still uncoiling from the ashes of the fires, which had gut-
ted much of the city. Pickett stood on Telegraph Hill and gazed
out at the miles of burned-out buildings and people with no
place to live milling about among the debris. He'd heard that

about 450 people had died in the earthquake. Based on what he saw, he was amazed that there were not more deaths.

In early 1907, Pickett's wanderings took him back to one of his favorite cities, Phoenix, Arizona, where his reputation had received a major boost in 1905. Drinking in the applause, Pickett recalled how great it had been two years before. Dave McClure had billed him as "Bulldog Pickett: the Dusky Demon—The Most Daring Cowboy Alive!" And the *Arizona Republican* had followed his cue and played up the event in bold type. "Bulldog Pickett Will Throw Steers With His Teeth Today at Eastlake Park," blared the Saturday edition.

Many of the spectators at Eastlake Park had asked Pickett if he was afraid of getting killed. Pickett told them getting killed should be the furtherest thing from a man's mind— whatever he was doing.

Pickett, according to the story, had promised to throw three steers with his teeth and to refund all the admission money if he failed to throw at least one. There was, of course, little chance Pickett and McClure would have to give the admission money back, barring some serious freak accident. The Dusky Demon downed the three steers promised and threw in a fourth for good measure.

The Sunday *Republican* commented: "One of the steers was as large an animal as was ever thrown by a cowboy in Phoenix . . . every person there is a walking advertisement for today's performance. Everyone was satisfied by the marvelous performance of the man Bill Pickett."

That same edition of the paper carried a feature article on Pickett that provided some interesting insight into the character of a man that, generally, has been regarded as just an extraordinary cowboy and showman, a physical man, not given to much thinking. The story bore the headline: "Bulldog Pickett a Fatalist. Not Afraid of Being Killed Until His Time Comes."

Many of the spectators at Eastlake Park had asked Pickett if he was afraid of getting killed. Pickett told them getting killed should be the farthest thing from a man's mind—whatever he was doing.

> I'm promised for this world just so long, and when I go, that will be the end of it . . . I'm thirty-four. I've lived as long as the average man . . . and have been throwing steers with my teeth for sixteen years. Sometime I suppose, I'll make a mistake . . . a fatal mistake . . . and it will be all over.

The bulldogger was an even bigger hit in Phoenix the second time around. He drew both those who had seen him perform before and wanted to see his act again, and those who had missed it the first time in Phoenix and wanted to find out if what they'd heard about it was true. It was hot in Phoenix, so hot that the dirt scorched his face and hands when he landed a steer. The sweat and dirt in his eyes sometimes blurred his vision. The discomfort of a sprained knee didn't help matters. But the roar of the crowd made Pickett impervious to pain and fatigue. Instead of the scheduled two performances, he put on three a day. It was an immensely successful engagement, perhaps too successful. The fanfare attracted the attention of fervent opponents of all cowboy sports.

It was during his 1907 visit to Arizona that Pickett had his first major head-on collision with the fruits of humane society lobbying efforts. Actually, all the furor had been stirred up over some instances of steers getting killed or hurt in roping and tying exhibitions, but it spilled over onto Pickett's act. The confrontation took place at the Don Luis Arena south of Bisbee. Arizona had passed a new law that year outlawing steer tying. That law did not spell out specifically that bulldogging was against the law, but Captain Harry Wheeler of the Arizona Rangers gave it a broad interpretation. Wheeler had a great reputation for enforcing unpopular laws. He was particularly hard on violations of gambling laws.

Although gambling was popular with most Arizonans, the more respectable ones wanted gambling (and the prostitution they associated with it) eliminated from the state. The Arizona legislature responded with curbs on games of chance (other than poker in public places, of course) and prohibitions against women and minors in saloons. In less than a year, Wheeler was able to report to the governor that "public gambling is not indulged anywhere," although there were a few underground roulette and faro games the Rangers would have very little chance of finding.

That same Arizona legislature passed a law against steer-tying contests that went into effect April 7, 1907. Its application to Pickett's act, which was touring the state at the time, was urged by an Arizona newspaper in these words: "To the morbid this has proven a most interesting feat, and crowds have gathered expressly to see this part of the performance."

Pickett was the featured performer with O. C. Nations and Clay McGonagill's steer-tying and bronco-busting show at that time. McGonagill was one of the greatest steer ropers in the country. During his career he won more than five hundred steer-roping contests. He was so good that when other ropers did exceptionally well, they often were applauded for "doing a McGonagill." Pickett was traveling in outstanding company and receiving top billing. Despite the new law, he continued to bulldog steers in Arizona for two weeks without interference. Then Wheeler struck. In *The Arizona Rangers*, Bill O'Neal gives this account:

> On Saturday, April 12, there was a performance at Don Luis, just south of Bisbee. A large number of "the morbid" gathered, but someone complained. Another performance was scheduled for Sunday at Don Luis, but Captain Harry Wheeler came up from Naco and, assisted by several other officers, halted the fun by threatening to arrest anyone who threw or roped any steers. The management had the foresight to gather "a large number of unbroken broncos," and the crowd had to be satisfied with an exhibition of bronco riding. The public had been protected from cruelty to animals in the guise of feats of skill.

The *Bisbee Review* smugly concluded: "There will be no more of it wherever there is an Arizona Ranger."

There were no Arizona Rangers in Dublin, Texas. So two weeks later, Pickett resumed busting down steers at an old settlers' reunion and elicited howls of delight from the throngs of the morbid there.

Pickett executed one of his most electrifying feats in El Paso, when he downed a full-grown male elk, with a huge crest of antlers. Those sharp accoutrements presented the greatest danger to the bulldogger. He could not simply jump off his horse and grab the sharp antlers. He'd get cut and lose his grip, and the animal might turn and skewer him with its cluster of horny knives. He could only jump off onto the animal's back and ride it until its legs tired. Then he clutched the antlers carefully close to the elk's forehead and dove sideways, toppling the beast. Biting, of course, was out of the question because of the antlers.

Pickett executed one of his most electrifying feats in El Paso, when he downed a full-grown male elk, with a huge crest of antlers.

Although the elk dogging did happen, reports that Pickett bulldogged buffaloes are open to question. Certainly he didn't make a habit of it, although he was in charge of the buffalo herd at the 101 Ranch and he often rode with the buffalo wagon in street parades when the 101 show hit a city. It is certain, however, that Pickett assisted in at least one buffalo dogging. That was when Guy Shultz, a show cowboy who made bulldogging buffalo his specialty, downed his first one. At the time, Shultz shared buffalo duty with Pickett between tours.

One day, while returning from another ranch, Shultz and Pickett found a secret homemade-whiskey still, and the owner gave them a gallon of the stuff to keep them quiet about it. They sipped on the whiskey during the ride back and their conversation turned to the problems Tom Mix and a movie company filming at the ranch were having trying to control the buffaloes they were using. They were watching a big herd of the brutes. Finally Schulz said:

"Bill, I believe I could bulldog one of those critters."

Amused, Pickett replied: "I don't believe I heard you right."

Schultz insisted, emboldened perhaps by the whiskey, but Pickett advised against it.

"A buffalo's got a head different from a steer, and his shoulders have a mean hump. It won't be like handling a steer. Are you sure you want to do this?" Pickett asked.

Schultz told Pickett how he planned to deal with the buffalo's anatomical peculiarities and asked the gutsy bulldogger to cut him out a bull and drive him down the fence to a nearby cottonwood tree.

Pickett was a marvelous horseman, and he had no problem separating the selected buffalo from the herd and maneuvering him to the chosen point. With Pickett riding as the hazer on the right side of the animal (to keep it moving in a straight line), Schultz galloped his horse on the buffalo's left side. Finally Schultz leaned off his horse, grabbed the buffalo's short curved horns, and catapulted forward out of the saddle. He hit the ground hopping, digging in his heels to slow down the 1,200-pound beast. Then he summoned all the strength in his 150-pound body and twisted the buffalo's head sideways. When the buffalo fell, Pickett was as excited as Schultz, and he complimented his companion on being the first to do that stunt.

Perhaps Pickett bulldogged some buffaloes after that, but it was not a common practice. Schultz, however, did make a name for himself by bulldogging buffaloes. Zack Miller fired Schultz, after the cowboy refused to put on an exhibition of buffalo dogging to collect a $500 bet. Schultz thought he was being cheated because the Millers stood to make thousands off his performance. Schultz did, however, bulldog buffaloes for a Chicago promoter for $3,000 a performance. The Miller brothers flew over the arena and observed the buffalo dogging from an airplane. They later rehired Schultz.

But that's getting ahead of the story.

Before proceeding to Jamestown, Virginia, the 101 Ranch Wild West Show launched its maiden voyage as a full-fledged professional traveling show in Chicago, where it wowed the crowds that jammed the Chicago Coliseum for thirteen days. Pickett was a sensation. He was one of only three cowboys introduced by name during the grand entrance. The others were Eddie Bolsford, chief of all cowboys; and George Elser, bronc buster and trick rider. Pickett was introduced as "Bill Pickett, the Dusky Demon, who throws steers with his teeth."

On the actual program, Pickett's act was placed next to last, just before the staged Indian attack on the wagon train, which was based on the performance that almost panicked the crowd at the National Editorial Convention show.

The idea, of course, was to heighten the suspense for the act most of the spectators had come to see. The audience was tantalized by the program note that said: "Bill Pickett, the Dusky Demon of Texas, a Negro who jumps from the back of a horse going full speed to that of a steer and then, grappling with the latter, throws it to the ground without using his hands in the operation."

That, of course, was stretching the truth a bit because Pickett did grab the steer's horns to control it and turn its head up to administer the kiss of the bulldog. But no one quibbled about that small detail after seeing the act. For some performances in Chicago, Pickett altered the act by having his hands tied behind his back before making the takedown.

The show proved to be such a hit in Chicago that the Millers made a quick trip back to the ranch, put together a second show, and sent it to Brighton Beach, New York, where it played to packed houses for six weeks. The Millers added Lucille Mulhall to the main show before proceeding to the Jamestown Exhibition.

At Jamestown, as in Chicago, Pickett was the showstopper. The 101 show was the most successful attraction of the three hundred years' celebration, thereby justifying President Theodore Roosevelt's prodding of the Jamestown Exhibition Committee to extend an invitation to the Millers.

Pickett was sidelined for a week during the Jamestown run due to injuries. A steer he dropped rolled over on him and pinned him down in an awkward position with the animal's full weight resting on his torso. Lon Sealy, who had been doing the bulldogging act with the Brighton Beach show filled in for him. At least Sealy tried. Sealy's performances left a lot to be desired, nevertheless some rodeo historians have credited him with being the first white bulldogger because of those efforts. Most accounts say Sealy wrestled a tame ox instead of a wild, ill-tempered, and unpredictable longhorn like those with which Pickett tangled.

Pickett was sidelined for a week during the Jamestown run due to injuries. A steer he dropped rolled over on him and pinned him down in an awkward position with the animal's full weight resting on his torso.

As soon as he could walk and ride Pickett was reinserted into the program. The audience, of course, was made aware that Pickett had suffered "severe injuries" but he "could not be restrained" any longer from getting back into the arena. TDR took in the show and was exhilarated by Pickett's act.

While at the exhibition, TDR toured the Negro Building, the so-called "Colored Exhibition" of Negro progress. After seeing Pickett's act it might have struck the president as paradoxical that the Negro Building contained nothing about Negroes like Pickett, those who helped conquer the West and shape its economy and culture.

You *Can* Go Home Again

ILL PICKETT AND THE 101 SHOW HAD ADDED
audiences in Richmond, Virginia, Atlanta, Georgia, and
Louisville, Kentucky, to the list of the thousands they had
thrilled and entertained by the time Pickett headed back
to Taylor, Texas. The bulldogger was ready to pause from his
wandering and stay home with his wife, Maggie, and their
seven daughters for a while.

However, this would be a different kind of homecoming,
because this was the last time Pickett would call Taylor home.
Maggie, the girls, and Pickett were moving. The Millers had
signed Pickett to a contract. The agreement provided that
Pickett would have both a job at the ranch and a place in the
show. The family also would be provided with a home, and
the children would be given jobs when they were old enough,
if they wanted them. It was the best of both worlds for
Pickett. It provided security for him and his family at a time

when economic uncertainty was the lot of most Americans, particularly blacks. Americans by the thousands were on the move seeking to better themselves, heading mainly north and west. The contract also provided a way for him to keep traveling and performing, things that were as essential to him as eating and sleeping.

Perhaps he should have discussed it with Maggie before signing on the dotted line, but he knew she wouldn't object strongly, if that was what he really wanted. Maggie was one of those "whither-thou-goest-I-will-go" kind of women. He knew that deep down inside she'd rather have him stay put and do something safe instead of being on the road so much and bulldogging. He knew how much it bothered her every time he came home battered and bruised and with cracked or broken bones. At thirty-seven, nearly every bone in his body had been cracked or broken at one time or another. But Maggie also knew how important performing and traveling were to her man, and she reconciled herself to living in a continual state of anxiety in order for him to pursue his work.

Pickett's constant traveling made for gratifying homecomings. He sometimes wondered which he enjoyed most—the going and doing, or the coming back and telling his family about where he'd been and what he'd done. They'd sit for hours, spellbound, listening to his tales. And when he drained himself of new stories, he'd have to retell the old ones again until each family member knew every detail by heart. This time he had to tell them about the 101 Ranch. He tried to do it justice, and sensing his enthusiasm, Maggie and the girls became excited about the move, too.

Actually Pickett had some very mixed feelings about leaving Taylor for good. After all, he'd called it home for about twenty years. He'd been born in nearby Travis County in Jenks-Branch, about thirty miles northwest of Austin, in 1870. He was the oldest of thirteen children born to Thomas Jefferson Pickett, a former slave, and Mary Pickett, who was part Cherokee. Shortly after Willie M. Pickett was born, the family moved to Austin, where Pickett completed the fifth grade. He also began learning the cowboy trade by working at odd jobs on ranches in or around Austin.

Pickett's constant traveling made for gratifying homecomings. He sometimes wondered which he enjoyed most — the going and doing or the coming back telling his family about where he'd been and what he'd done.

The family moved to Taylor when Bill was about eighteen years old. At the time Taylor had about three thousand residents and was a thriving railroad center in the middle of one of Texas's most fertile agricultural belts. Bill's cowboy skills enabled him to find work at ranches throughout the surrounding counties. He also picked cotton and did any other odd jobs he could find to supplement the family income.

Pickett knew just about everybody in and around Taylor. He'd worked for half of them or broke horses for them, or served with them in the National Guard.

About a year-and-a-half after the move to Taylor, Bill experienced a pivotal moment in his life. He met Maggie

Turner of Palestine. Maggie's father was a plantation owner named Sherman Turner. Her mother was one of his ex-slaves. At the time when Maggie and Bill met she was using her stepfather's name, Williams. Bill was totally captivated by Maggie. During his days apart from her, he carried the picture in his mind of her dark chocolate face, her almond-shaped, brown eyes, and her ropes of tar black shiny hair tumbling to her shoulders. And when he tasted the nectar of her plump, moist hennaed lips, he became a hopeless case. He knew from the moment he met her that he would have chosen her from among all the women in the world. Bill pursued Maggie with a gentle and shy relentlessness until she caught him. The chase ended on December 2, 1890, when they married. Their union produced nine children. The two males died before reaching their first birthdays. The seven surviving girls—Nannie, Bessie, Leona, Willie, Kleora Virginia, Almarie, and Alberdia—were precious living jewels to him, and he worked tirelessly to keep them housed, fed, and clothed. He hunted and fished to supplement the family's meat supply, sometimes using just a knife. And he often took his older children along with him on forays into the woods.

Bill pursued Maggie with a gentle and shy relentlessness until she caught him. The chase ended on December 2, 1890, when they married. Their union produced nine children.

As he pondered the move to Oklahoma, Pickett's mind flashed back to the days when he and his brothers were in the bronc-busting business. Ben and he did most of the taming. It was rough, dangerous, exhausting work. Unlike the rides of a few seconds in cowboy roundup contests, the actual breaking of a wild horse sometimes took all day or several days of bone-jarring, butt-bruising struggle. It meant being thrown off repeatedly and the risk of being kicked, bitten, or pancaked by a rolling horse. The Picketts were good at the work, and they had a reputation for not mistreating the horses.

There was one horse in particular Pickett would never forget. He almost gave up on that animal. It was a big three-year-old chestnut that tried to kick him in the head when he approached him with a bridle. It took two of them to get the horse saddled, and when Pickett straddled him, the horse leaped a good six feet in the air, pawing and shrieking like a devil out of hell. He kicked, he bucked, he spun around in circles. When he threw Pickett off, he kept running around bucking, trying to shed the saddle. When Pickett got on him again, it was more of the same. The horse was determined not to be ridden. He tried to roll on his side and crush Pickett, but the cowboy was too quick and savvy for that. He tried to bite and got a taste of the reins across his sensitive nose. The battle raged for hours, on-again, off-again, man, horse, and flying dirt.

Some men might have taken a whip to a horse so mean, but not Bill Pickett. He was as determined to ride that horse as that horse was determined not to be ridden. That horse was

> *It took two of them to get the horse saddled, and when Pickett straddled him, the horse leaped a good six feet in the air, pawing and shrieking like a devil out of hell.*

like life. It had its ups and downs, but if you meet it on its own terms and hang in there you will prevail. That's how Pickett thought about that situation. It wasn't right to whip a horse into submission. The challenge was to break the animal without breaking its spirit. So Pickett took the bruises and the bumps, and in the end he succeeded in gentling the chestnut. But that horse left a lasting impression on him, and its memory would come flashing back one fateful day.

The bronc-busting business was not enough to support a family by itself. Bill and his brothers continued to work at ranches, and before long Bill was bringing in money from his bulldogging exhibitions around the state.

SUDDENLY BLIND

A religious man, Bill Pickett was a deacon at the Taylor Baptist Church and had a reputation for being a poor singer and not much given to praying in public. His faith, however, was strong, and it sustained him through one of the most mysterious and frightening experiences of his life. One day near the turn of the century, just when things were beginning to look bright for Pickett, darkness descended blacker than a moonless midnight in a swamp on Bill Pickett. He unexplainably lost his eyesight.

Perhaps it was the delayed effects of a head injury or an infection. No one could figure out why, at thirty years of age, Pickett became blind as a bat. For a man who had been so active all his life it was the ultimate torture—to be almost helpless like that. Nannie had to lead him around to all places that were unfamiliar to him. He could feel his way around the house after a time, and he could groom the horses in the barn by feel once he was escorted there.

It was perhaps during that dark year of his life that Pickett developed his standard fatalistic response when confronted with adversity and danger: "What's gonna happen, gonna happen."

The family prayed continuously for understanding and help. Then a year later, when they had all but reconciled themselves to Pickett's being blind for the rest of his life, the darkness that had descended upon the bulldogger suddenly and mysteriously lifted. On that day the words of

No one could figure out why, at thirty years of age, Pickett became blind as a bat.

the hymn "Amazing Grace" acquired a new depth of meaning to Bill Pickett when he sang, or more precisely, tried to sing: "I was blind, but now I see."

Chapter Six

························

Once upon a Time
in the Wild West

❧

I T RAINED. THEN IT RAINED. AND THEN . . .
it rained some more. Buckets full. Sheets of mud-making,
audience-diminishing, profit-killing water poured from the
skies. Bullfrogs ribbetted: Enough! Enough! For most of the
first six weeks of its first full-fledged tour in 1908, the Miller
Brothers 101 Ranch Real Wild West Show's tracks were
bedeviled by downpours. The moisture caused operating cash
to dry up and drove the Millers to serious thoughts of chucking
the whole idea of a traveling Wild West show. Surely Mother
Nature was trying to tell them something. Wild West shows
were a high risk business under the best of circumstances, but
this most-strange foul and unnatural weather was a killer.

By the time the Miller brothers decided to plunge whole
hog into the Wild West show business, scores of shows had hit
the trail blazed by William Frederick Cody, a.k.a. Buffalo Bill
Cody, with varying degrees of success and failure. Most of the

impresarios of western heritage show business harbored visions of dazzling the nation and popping the eyes of European royalty out of their noble sockets, just as Buffalo Bill had done with his shows. Some came close, but most had to settle for just trying to hang on from town to town.

Zack Mulhall, a fellow Oklahoma rancher, had done well before he got into some difficulties with the law. He was charged with attempted murder for shooting a man during an altercation. Joe and Zack Miller had previously participated in the Mulhall show in Madison Square Garden in 1905.

Another of the more notable on-again, off-again shows was Pawnee Bill's Historic Wild West. It went under in 1889, partially as a result of an abortive European tour and partially due to a billing war that happened during a tour of the South involving the Buffalo Bill show. But the Pawnee Bill show would rebound many times with new partners and new acts.

Pawnee Bill's real name was Gordon W. Lillie. A kind of western legend like Buffalo Bill, Lillie had been a trapper, a cowboy, a secretary, and a teacher at the Pawnee Agency. He got into show business when he served as interpreter for the Pawnees for the original Cody and Carver Wild West of 1883, which had started the whole Wild West show proliferation.

Actually, Buffalo Bill lit the Wild West show fire in 1882, when, after a successful stint in vaudeville, he returned to his hometown of North Pointe, Nebraska. There he found that the town had no plans for a Fourth of July celebration. Inasmuch as Cody was the person in town most concerned about that, he was given the job of organizing the event. Out of that celebration was born his Wild West show, which would spend two decades crisscrossing the nation and Europe several times and be the model for scores of imitators.

In 1908, while the 101 Ranch Wild West Show was sloshing through rain and the mud in the great plains, about three dozen shows were on the road, had been on the road, or had quit and reemerged as a new show. Among them were: Broncho John, Famous Western Horseman and His Corps of Expert Horsemen; Buckskin Ben's Wild West and Dog and Pony Show; Buckskin Bill's Wild West; Buckskin Joe's Realistic Wild West; Buffalo and Wild West; Buffalo Bill and Dr. Carver's Wild West; Buffalo Bill's Wild West; Coup and Carver's Wild West; Colonel Frederick J. Cummin's Indian Congress; Cummin's Wild West and Indian Congress; Fargo and Company; Adam Forepaugh's New and Greatest All-Feature Show and Wild West Combination; Luella Forepaugh-Fish Wild West; Gabriel Brothers Champion Long Distance Riders Wild West; Hart and Schofield Indian Show; Indian Bill's Wild West; Indian Bill's Wild West and Cole and Rogers Circus Combined; Kemp Sisters Wild West; Kennedy Brothers Wild West; King and Franklin's Wild West; P. Matally's Wild West; O'Dell's Famous Hippodrome and F. J. McCarthy's Arizona Wild West; Walter C. Sharp's Troop of Rough Riders; Capt. Ed Senchal's Wild West; Skakel and Martin; Stowe and Long's Circus Menagerie; Sutton's American Wild West and Roman Hippodrome and Buck Taylor's Wild West; Texas Bill's Wild West; and Cole Younger and Frank James Wild West.

Faced with all that competition, and rain to boot, things looked pretty bleak for the new show business outfit from Oklahoma. The tour had kicked off promisingly in Ponca City, Oklahoma. The mayor of that city declared a holiday and the whole city turned out for the grand parade that featured two hundred performers. Heading the cast were Pickett and Tom Mix. Other cowboys and cowgirls included Guy Weadick, Vester Pegg, Rose Scott, Julia Allen, Vern Tantlinger, Dan Cox, William Allenberry, Charles Lipton, George Elsor, and George Hooker.

Faced with all that competition, and rain to boot, things looked pretty bleak for the new show business outfit from Oklahoma.

Although Pickett is the only black 101 performer most people have heard about, George Hooker was part black, part Mexican. He was a fantastic roper and rider. Zack Miller once said of Hooker: "Maybe that wild, ripping yell that George Hooker cut loose with put the spirit in it (a show rehearsal). That big yellow-skinned half-Negro, half-Mexican had a holler that could split an eardrum two city blocks away; and Hooker was always plenty willing to give it out."

After Ponca City, the rain came and stayed with the tour most of the time through Kansas and Illinois. It even rained on the parade in Chicago. The constant wet weather not only caused low attendance, it also set the stage for numerous accidents and injuries to performers and livestock from skidding on the wet dirt. The performers usually finished their acts covered with mud. Pickett was fortunate to avoid serious injuries during the monsoons.

During one performance in Chicago, Pickett's horse slipped, causing him to miss the steer's back. Pickett grabbed the steer's front hoof, but the steer jerked it away and kept going. He clutched at the back hoof, but he couldn't maintain his grip on that one either. In a last desperate effort to stop the steer, he grabbed its tail. The steer's momentum yanked him to his feet. Pickett pulled with all his strength to stop the steer. But the animal would have none of that. He churned ahead as hard as he could. Pickett leaned back at a 45-degree angle, and his boots cut through the mud like a plow. The steer gave a great exertion, Pickett came flying forward. He managed to take two long strides before launching himself and landing on the steer's neck. He grabbed the horns, dug in his heels, and twisted the steer's head back and up. He threw wide his arms and fell back, taking the steer down with him. The splash they created covered both man and steer with mud. The small audience clapped its appreciation, but the sound was hollow in the almost-empty tent.

. . . in Chicago, Pickett's horse slipped, causing him to miss the steer's back. Pickett grabbed the steer's front hoof, but the steer jerked it away and kept going. He clutched at the back hoof, but he couldn't maintain his grip on that one either. In a last desperate effort to stop the steer, he grabbed its tail.

In Joplin, Missouri, when the show had tumbled $30,000 in the hole (a ton of money in those days), Edward Arlington, the Millers' partner, broached the possibility of giving up to Joe Miller. Arlington, who owned the rolling stock, had previously been with Barnum and Bailey's Circus and Pawnee Bill's Historic Wild West. He told Miller he was out of cash and had no way to raise any more.

Miller replied: "Eddie, all our neighbors prophesied we'd go broke in show business. Maybe they're right. But I figure this loss is just like a little drought at home with cattle. I'm willing to put twenty thousand more into it. Take the show where you think it's best to go, but don't get farther than this twenty thousand will (sic) get it back. Then if we go under, we'll just mark it off as a bad deal, like maybe two thousand cattle had starved out and died. And we'll forget it."

Very soon thereafter came a moment when Miller cursed the day he had given Arlington that geographical blank check. That happened in Fergus Falls, Minnesota, a postage-stamp-sized town that struck Miller as a mistake the instant he laid eyes on it. The rain finally had let up in St. Paul. Still they made expenses by just a hair. The last place they needed to go after that was Fergus Falls, Minnesota. It had to be the end of the trail. He couldn't figure for the life of him why Arlington would have booked the show into a nowhere place like Fergus Falls.

The town was about one hundred seventy-five miles, as the crow flies, from Minneapolis on the Otter Tail River. In 1908, that tiny speck of habitation in its vast, empty landscape looked much farther away from Minneapolis and looked very small to Joe Miller, Zack Miller, and Bill Pickett. When Pickett looked out the train window and saw the small row of buildings and the one path that (in a stretch) could be called a street, he couldn't believe they were actually supposed to put on a show there. But someone had been there before them putting up posters announcing they were coming and his name was on them big as life: "Bill Pickett, the Dusky Demon." He just wondered why.

Zack Miller needed a drink. But he needed to put some food on his stomach before he got down to the serious drinking he expected he would need to do to get through the Fergus Falls debacle. But when he went into a restaurant for breakfast and saw only half a dozen people on the street, he lost his appetite. He sat in the restaurant for about an hour transfixed in gloom, and sipping his coffee now and then. He sent his food back untouched. Finally, he went outside only to be shocked to his socks by an amazing sight. He couldn't believe it. Hordes of people were converging on the town, coming from all directions. Indians, as well as whites. On foot. On horseback. In wagons. Isolated people starved for entertainment were thronging to see the big show that had wandered into their little farming community.

The sight cheered Zack Miller so much that he went back into the restaurant and wolfed down two orders of bacon and eggs.

Seeing the crowd pouring into town, Arlington immediately doubled the admission price from fifty cents to a dollar and tacked on another dollar for reserved seats. He raised the sideshow admission from ten cents to a quarter. Despite the ticket prices, all performances sold out. They had to pile hay in the aisles to seat extra people. Indians were allowed through the back gate, where blankets, furs, and hides were accepted from those who had no money.

The big tent was so crammed with people for all performances that some of the wilder horses had to be held out of the show to keep spectators from getting hurt. Horses and steers frequently got loose and had to be retrieved before they got into the audience. Usually, there was a buffer area to allow room to catch the animals. But at Fergus Falls, the big tent was so packed they had to seat people right down on the edge of ringside.

Pickett brought the Fergus Falls folks to their feet during his first performance when he "hoolihaned" a steer. (This means after jumping from the horse to the steer, the cowboy knocks down the steer without twisting its head.) He landed with such force on the neck and horns of the steer that the animal fell forward and turned a somersault. When the dazed longhorn scrambled to its feet, Pickett leaped on its horns, corkscrewed its head around, chomped his teeth into its sensitive nose, and did a backward lay-out. The skull-rattling crescendo of hand-clapping, war-whooping, and shrieks of delight were music to Pickett's soul, after so many waterlogged performances before nearly empty stands.

Buoyed by the Fergus Falls financial bonanza the show went on to Calgary, Ontario, Canada, where Pickett was a familiar figure and again received thunderous ovations. Then they went to Winnipeg, where crowds were so large and enthusiastic that police had to be pressed into service to help control them. By the time they left Canada, the show was out of debt and $20,000 in the black. The rain was gone, and a financial rainbow had appeared. During the next five months, the show visited eleven states. Although there was some more rain in Montana and a train wreck in North Dakota, the tour overall was a success.

After a stop in Brownsville, Texas, in early December, the Millers decided to take the show into Mexico. Pickett did not go with them. He was sent back to the 101 Ranch to help round up stock, recover from various bumps, bruises, and lacerations, and spend some time with Maggie and the kids.

Pickett stopped off in Fort Worth on the way home for the opening of the city's new Cowtown Coliseum, the finest facility of its kind in those days. Pickett again was a sensation there.

The Picketts, who had lived briefly on the ranch after relocating from Texas, had since moved to Ponca City, about nine miles away. That way the kids could attend a special school set up in a church for the benefit of the handful of black families in the community. It was good to be back with Maggie and the girls. He had more adventures than ever stored up, and he so enjoyed telling and being the center of their attention while they drank in every word like thirsty fields sopping up rain. He also had a lot of aches and pains for Maggie to fuss over. But it was not just because he was tired and hurting and wanted to be with his family that Pickett chose not to make the Mexico tour. He had an inexplicably bad feeling about Mexico. It was as though he was being warned constantly in his dreams not to go there. He didn't know why. He'd performed in Mexico several times and had always been well received. He spoke pretty good Spanish and got along well with Mexicans there, as well as in the United States.

Still, in his dreams he saw horrible, black, horned, shadowy figures, and bloody swords, and a coffin with a Spanish word on it he did not understand. Sometimes the coffin opened, and he saw his face in it. The horned forms would cover him, and he'd wake up drenched with sweat.

Still, in his dreams he saw horrible, black, horned, shadowy figures, and bloody swords, and a coffin with a Spanish word on it he did not understand.

The bad dreams stopped when the show departed for Mexico without him. But they returned when the word came a couple of weeks later that the show was in trouble and it needed him. Not only had the crowds been disappointing, but the show was about to get into big trouble with the Mexican authorities. There was a law down there against advertising an act that was not in the show. The 101 promotional material prominently promised the Dusky Demon and bulldogging, and if he didn't show up soon, somebody might go to jail.

Despite the troubling portents, Pickett had no choice but to go to Mexico. He hugged and kissed his family and boarded the train south for the border, thinking: "What's gonna happen, gonna happen."

Chapter Seven

Toro! Toro! Toro!:
Dance with a Killer Bull

I T WAS UNUSUALLY WARM FOR DECEMBER 23 in Mexico City, or maybe it just seemed that way because of all the excitement in the air that day in 1908. From towns and villages miles away, in all directions men, women, and children, rich, poor, and in-between streamed into the city to join with local residents in celebrating the birth of the Lord Jesus Christ and the death of Bill Pickett.

The black Yankee's torn and bleeding corpse—impaled on the horns of Bonito—would be a wonderful gift to the people of Mexico, who had suffered far too many insults from the arrogant and overbearing North Americans. Pickett's broken and lacerated body, his red blood oozing into the gray sand of the arena and congealing into black mud was the price they demanded as compensation for the slap in the face he and his bosses had delivered to Mexico. When that price was paid, the festivities leading up to Christmas would begin, and everyone would have a joyous time.

It had all started one evening at the Cafe Colon, a favorite haunt of bullfighters and aficionados. The Miller Brothers and Arlington Wild West Show had been in Mexico City for a week, and it was drawing respectable crowds, despite the depressed economic conditions in the country at the time. After several rounds of beers, some of the bullfighters began boasting that any of them could do what Pickett did to those docile steers and generally making light of Pickett's act. Colonel Joe Miller finally got his craw overfilled with the braggadocio and challenged the bullfighters to put up or shut up. There were no takers.

A couple of days later, however, an article, instigated by Miller, appeared in the *Mexico City Herald* that generated a furor. The article asserted that Bill Pickett's act was far more daring and exciting than the best Mexican bullfight. The boast hit Mexico City like a broom swatting a nest of hornets. *El Heraldo*, the main competitor to the *Herald*, fired back the claim that any bullfighter could put on a better show than Bill Pickett at his best. Joe Miller then ran an ad in the *Herald* that said Pickett could throw two steers quicker than two Mexican bullfighters could throw one.

Still there were no takers, but insults continued to be traded back and forth in the newspapers. A response came, however, when Miller offered to give one thousand pesos to charity if any bullfighter could throw a steer the same size as one Pickett would throw. Manolo Bienvenida, one of the most famous and admired bullfighters of the day, accepted

71

Toro! Toro! Toro!: Dance with a Killer Bull

the challenge on the condition that the contest be held out of the public eye. Such an exhibition, after all, was beneath the dignity of a bullfighter.

Bienvenida, however, did not show for the bull-throwing contest. He sent a note explaining that he had been forbidden to do it by the bullfighters union and officials of the arena where he performed.

Ever the promoter, Miller seized upon Bienvenida's no-show to expand upon the theme of Pickett's valor and to suggest that the bullfighters were not as brave as they led people to believe. He poured salt into the wounds by making those statements in the *Herald*. His boasting both boosted attendance at the 101 shows and riled the local populace to the boiling point.

The bullfighters responded by wagering five thousand pesos that Pickett could not stay on a fighting bull for five minutes. Miller accepted without conferring with Pickett. When he did get around to asking Pickett if he thought he could do it, Miller had no doubt about what the cowboy's response would be. Pickett did not disappoint him.

By then, of course, the bet had become the ammunition of a newspaper war between the *Herald* and *El Heraldo*, with Miller holding forth in the former and the bullfighters in the latter. The duel of the newspapers greatly increased attendance at the Wild West show and set the stage for the December 23 moment of truth.

El Toro, the new concrete-and-steel bullring, was crammed to the point of suffocation with twenty-five thousand people, including the president of Mexico, Porfirio Diaz. Not another body could be shoehorned into the stands. Outside the arena the crush was just as bad. The noise was deafening; a thunderous roar, punctuated by frequent choruses of "Muerte, Muerte" and the happy, contradictory strains of mariachi fiddles, trumpets, and tenor incantations. The crowd outside the arena swayed to the rhythm of the music, dancing en masse because there was no room to dance individually. It was almost Christmas Eve and Bill Pickett was going to die. He was going to die because he deserved to die, because any man who would do such a stupid thing deserved to be ground into the dirt and trampled the way Bonito was going to do to him. And they were happy about that—happy and impatient.

It was unpardonable for Pickett, a performer of clownish stunts, to boast and bet that he could subdue a beautiful, brave bull the way he did the lowly beef cattle he toppled in his act. True, it was impressive the way he jumped off his horse onto the bull and finally threw the animal down and held him still biting him in the lip and falling backward. It was quite an act, a dangerous one even, but in their view it was not even close to being comparable to the death-defying work of a matador. To suggest that it was bordered on blasphemy.

Any man who would dare such a *loco* thing as trying to throw a fighting bull deserved the certain, excruciating death that was in store for Pickett. For his service to Mexico in disemboweling the egotistical black cowboy, some said, Bonito should be allowed to live out his days without ever having to

73

Toro! Toro! Toro!: Dance with a Killer Bull

go into the ring again. He should be given his own herd of the finest cows to service, and breed more brave bulls like himself.

The cry went up, "Bonito! Bonito! Bonito!"

As he watched the crowd shoving and pushing into the stands, Pickett was vaguely amused by their enthusiasm and somewhat excited by it himself. It always fired him up to see the spectators waiting for his performance. He knew that people liked to watch performers risk getting seriously hurt or killed. Part of every spectator was afraid for the man taking that risk. Yet mixed with that concern for the safety of the performer was the desire to be there to witness a tragedy firsthand. Pickett had always understood and identified with those ambivalent feelings in his audiences. He sometimes took more risks than necessary in order to satisfy their need for the secondhand experience of danger.

It wasn't until he saw the coffin that Pickett came to the full realization that this audience had no worry for his safety at all. They had come to see him die.

It wasn't until he saw the coffin that Pickett came to the full realization that this audience had no worry for his safety at all. They had come to see him die. There was a Spanish word emblazoned in red on the side of the black coffin, "El Pincharino." He asked one of the Mexican boys who had hired on with the show what it meant. The boy stammered, not wishing to be the bearer of such a message. But Pickett insisted.

"What kind of name are they calling me, Pedro?" Pickett asked.

"It means . . . I think it means one who has been run through by the horns of a bull," said Pedro.

So they did have him dead already. They had made a coffin for him, and they were just waiting to put his bloody, broken body in it and plant it in some unmarked grave somewhere. The sight of the coffin upset Pickett. It didn't scare him, but it did set something gnawing on his insides. He went over to Colonel Joe Miller and asked him point-blank what would happen to his body if he got killed in the arena. Miller was a little taken aback and did not respond immediately. The fact was that the possibility of Bill Pickett getting killed had really never occurred to him. He just took it for granted that Pickett was invulnerable.

"What I would like," said Pickett, "if that happens is for you to take me back to Oklahoma, back home, near my family. Bury me deep in hard ground, so the coyotes can't scratch up my bones," said Pickett.

Miller assured Pickett that he would comply with his wish. Then he inquired if Pickett were having second thoughts and if he wanted to call the whole thing off. He knew better, of course. He believed Pickett was unafraid of anything that walked on four hooves.

Pickett said they'd have to tie him to keep him from going out into that ring, which reconfirmed Miller's estimate of Pickett's guts.

Of course, Miller had gotten a little worried when they went to look at the bulls from which Pickett's combatant would be picked. They were some fearsome beasts, far different

75

Toro! Toro! Toro!: Dance with a Killer Bull

from the breed of bovine Pickett had been accustomed to man-handling. They came from mean stock, having descended from the wild bulls of the Iberian Peninsula. Their ancestors were bulls so strong, agile, and fierce that they had killed lions in the Roman circuses.

Modern fighting bulls were carefully bred and nurtured to preserve and enhance the natural mean streak in their species. Only those who made the grade for mean-ness ever made it to the bullrings of the bullfighting world. Those deemed not fierce enough became steaks and rump roasts. Bonito, the animal the bullfighters picked for Pickett to wrestle, had made the grade with plenty of room to spare.

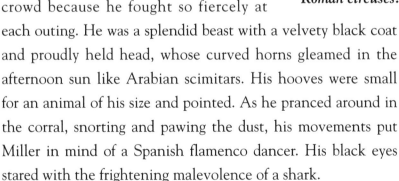

They came from mean stock, having descended from the wild bulls of the Iberian Peninsula. Their ancestors were bulls so strong, agile and fierce that they had killed lions in the Roman circuses.

Bonito had already killed men and horses, and his life had been spared by the crowd because he fought so fiercely at each outing. He was a splendid beast with a velvety black coat and proudly held head, whose curved horns gleamed in the afternoon sun like Arabian scimitars. His hooves were small for an animal of his size and pointed. As he pranced around in the corral, snorting and pawing the dust, his movements put Miller in mind of a Spanish flamenco dancer. His black eyes stared with the frightening malevolence of a shark.

Miller wondered then if he had not let himself get swept up in his own bravado and put Pickett unnecessarily in peril of his life. After all, he'd concluded the bet before he even mentioned it to the cowboy. He just assumed that Pickett had the pluck to try almost anything. He wouldn't have blamed Pickett if he'd wanted to back out, although he knew it was too late for that. He offered Pickett a drink. The cowboy took a couple of long swigs of the sour mash, not because he needed it to steady his nerves, but because he liked the taste of the stuff, the tingle on his tongue and in his throat. He fetched the stub of a stogie out of his shirt pocket and relit it. A slug of good whiskey and a good cigar were two of Pickett's greatest pleasures in life, although he never drank to excess.

"No, I'm not scared of that bull, Colonel Joe," said Pickett. "I'm really kind of anxious to get on with the show. I just wanted it understood what was to be done with me in case something unexpected happened."

He was being truthful. Even after seeing the bulls up close and personal, Pickett wasn't scared. He'd seen bullfights before, seen how the bulls plowed into the poor horses of the guys with the spears. He'd even seen a bullfighter gored once. And a chilling sight it was. More often, though, it was the bull that died. The whole show centered upon the death of the bull. The bullfighter was cheered if he did his killing with daring and style.

But this crowd had come to cheer for the bull. They had come to see Pickett die. And that was hard for the cowboy to take, the thought that those people were that much against him. For the adoration of a crowd, he'd take any chance. He was just that much of a showman. Show business was in his

77

Toro! Toro! Toro!: Dance with a Killer Bull

blood. That was the thing that compelled him to leave his family for such long stretches of time. It was in his blood as certainly as the urge to kill surged through the veins of the fighting bulls.

Pickett was slow to anger, but the crowd's hostility made him mad and increased his desire to beat the bull and spit in the faces of those calling for his death. He'd make them bury their blood lust in the coffin they'd made for him. He'd spoil their Christmas wish for the gift of his death.

A sudden hush fell over the arena, then rolling murmurs of confusion. The crowd was reacting to a large sign that was being held up by the El Toro officials. It said in Spanish that Bonito had been withdrawn from the feature event of the day. None of them could figure out what that meant. Were they to be deprived of the spectacle they had looked forward to for so many days? Had the arrogant black North American shown his true color? So many had come to see the Pincharino get what was coming to him. How could they do that to them? Someone would pay for this. Someone would die. The moment demanded blood, and they would not be denied. A roar went up from the crowd that was like the bellowing of a herd of enraged bulls, a cacophonous eruption of boos, curses, and threats.

What the crowd did not know was that the contest had been halted by the governor of the Federal District of Mexico. The governor had yielded to the appeals of some prominent American women residing in Mexico, who begged him to save Pickett's life by stopping the contest with Bonito. Having secured that pledge, the women went away content that no American would be sacrificed on the horns of a fighting bull.

No one wanted to explain that to the enraged crowd. Trying to do so would have served only to make a bad situation worse. The way through the horns of the dilemma, however, lay in the governor's decree that created it. That order said specifically that Pickett was not to grapple with Bonito. It did not say that he could not try to subdue another bull. Miller spotted the loophole first and pointed it out to the *El Toro* officials. The interpretation was carried to the box where the governor and President Diaz were seated.

What the crowd did not know was that the contest had been halted by the governor of the Federal District of Mexico. The governor had yielded to the appeals of some prominent American women residing in Mexico, who begged him to save Pickett's life by stopping the contest with Bonito.

Just at the point where it appeared that the crowd was about to tear the place apart, another sign went up. It said that instead of Bonito, Pickett would be matched against Frijoli Chiquita. Again, there was a hush thick enough to be cut with a machete, while the crowd went through an exercise of collective comprehension. Then an explosion of jubilation rattled the arena. Yes, Frijoli Chiquita (Spanish for "Little Beans") would be a fine substitute for Bonito. The bull got his name from the spots on his rump. Like Bonito he had killed men and horses, and his life had been spared for his bravery.

79

Toro! Toro! Toro!: Dance with a Killer Bull

"*Viva Frijoli Chiquita! Viva Frijoli Chiquita! Viva Frijoli Chiquita!*" The crowd was on its feet chanting in unison.

Pickett had noticed the bull with the spots when they went to the corral to pick one out. That would have been his pick if he had been one of the Mexicans, because of the bull's extra large neck and his horns that seemed a bit longer than most fighting bulls. Those horns had deadly, needlelike tips. The speckled bull was as menacing as any creature Pickett had ever seen, but the cowboy was not afraid. Something inside him ached for the challenge, a challenge that had been pushed upon him by others.

"*Viva El Toro! Viva Frijoli Chiquita! Viva El Toro! Viva Frijoli Chiquita!*" they chanted in unison. Then someone with a loud, piercing voice yelled, "*Recuerda bienvenida!*"

The chorus of blood lust was accompanied by the drumbeats of stamping feet and the castanets of clapping hands.

Joe Miller ordered the show to proceed. The Mexicans were in no mood for the foreplay. They booed the bronc riding, the calf roping, and every other act offered. They had come for blood, and they were tired of waiting. The arena vibrated with the drumbeats of stamping feet. They were impatient for the slaughter, and the fever of their blood lust turned the winter evening into torrid summer.

Sensing the crowd's threatening mood, Joe Miller abruptly shortened the program, and the announcer proclaimed the grand event of the evening, a contest between man and bull, featuring the Dusky Demon, *El Ferroz Fenomeno Negro de*

Oklahoma, Bill Pickett, and the brave bull Frijoli Chiquita. There was a flourish of trumpets, and Pickett, mounted on his favorite horse, Spradley, advanced into the arena. A momentary hush ensued. Then the crowd erupted into a roar of boos, the most malevolent sound the cowboy had ever heard. It sounded to him like a choir of devils come out of hell to try to scare him to death.

He had never faced a crowd like that. Always before they had been with him, although some may have secretly longed for the thrill of being there when he got killed. But all of these people wanted to see him die. It was confusing and disappointing. He knew it was not a racial thing. He had performed before and been cheered in Mexico, even before he joined up with the 101. Some of his relatives had chosen to live in Mexico to escape persecution and discrimination in the United States. Of course, he could understand their being upset by the thought that someone would dare to belittle their national sport. But he could not understand how their hurt feelings could drive them to want to see him suffer a horrible death.

The thought of their hatred steeled Pickett's determination to succeed. He would draw strength from the heat of their anger and win their approval in the end for his display of strength and courage. While the crowd chanted for his death, Pickett prayed to his God for the power to meet the challenge and return to Oklahoma to see his wife and daughters.

From the other side of the arena the sound of firecrackers and Frijoli Chiquita's demonic bellowing could be heard.

Vaqueros were tormenting the bull to intensify his rage. The chute opened, and the bull bounded into the arena like a speeding steam engine bolting out of a tunnel. The crowd was in a frenzy.

"Viva El Toro! Viva Frijoli Chiquita!" The din was deafening.

Four other cowboys rode into the arena to try to steer the bull in a straight line so that Pickett could ride alongside him and jump onto the animal's back. That further inflamed the crowd, which had been led to believe that Pickett would face the bull alone. Of course, the audience did not take into account the fact that a matador had the assistance of a picador and other bullfighters to place the banderillas and weaken the bull's neck and shoulders.

In the end, however, Pickett had to confront the bull alone. The other cowboys proved useless against the quick, agile fighting bull that could turn on a nickel and give change. They left the arena after one cowboy's horse was gored in the flank. Then Frijoli Chiquita charged at Pickett and Spradley. The horse adroitly sidestepped the bull's ferocious rush. The force of that charge was such that Frijoli Chiquita rose up on his hind legs when he missed. He swerved again, and again Spradley evaded the lethal, needle-pointed horns. But Spradley was too far away from the bull for Pickett to jump onto Frijoli Chiquita.

Because the bull could turn so quickly, there appeared to be no way for Pickett to get close enough to him without getting his favorite horse killed. Pickett had seen what happened to the picadors' horses in bullfights. Those poor horses had heavy padding on their sides, but Pickett had heard the agonized screams of the wretched horses when the bulls struck them, and he knew they were being broken up inside. Of course, the doomed horses were bound for the slaughterhouse anyway. Pickett wanted Spradley to live because he loved him as much as a man could love an animal.

For two minutes that must have seemed like two hours to the frenzied mob, the mounted horseman and the bull danced a lovely and lethal ballet of charge and evade. The marvelous display of horsemanship would have been much more appreciated in another setting. To those in the stands that day it seemed like a dance of cowardice. They booed so loudly that the sound was like the bellowing of a herd of angry bulls.

Finally Pickett turned Spradley abruptly and raced behind the barrier to confer with Miller. The crowd went wild, thinking Pickett was giving up. While the spectators were throwing a collective tantrum of screamed threats and foot stomping, Frijoli Chiquita raced around the ring, pawing the gray sand and ramming into the walls.

Pickett, meanwhile, was imploring Miller to get him another horse so he would not have to sacrifice Spradley to the bull's rage. The horse was precious to Pickett because he had saved its life after it picked up a big splinter in its chest and the wound had become infected. While Pickett begged Miller for another horse the crowd grew surlier and surlier and the bull grew meaner and meaner.

83

Toro! Toro! Toro!: Dance with a Killer Bull

Miller told Pickett to go back into the arena and finish the job, "or we're all gonna get killed."

Reluctantly Pickett headed Spradley back into ring, and the bull charged immediately. Spradley shifted his legs to sidestep, but Pickett drew back hard on the reins and held him in place. Frijoli Chiquita drove his long, sharp horns up to his forehead in Spradley's rump. The poor horse screamed in agony and slumped down behind. Frijoli Chiquita had extracted his horns and was preparing to lunge again, but at that instant Pickett vaulted backward from the saddle and grabbed the bull by those blood-soaked horns.

The bull heaved and shook with all its might, but Picket held on. The bull raced around the arena, dragging Pickett and slamming him against the walls, but Pickett stuck like glue.

Because of the gore, it was hard to get a good grip on the horns. But it was a matter of life and death, and Pickett summoned superhuman strength from somewhere to secure his hold. The crowd was ecstatic, celebrating already. It would only be a few seconds. Frijoli Chiquita would shake Pickett loose like a feather with one shrug of his great neck and then skewer him through the bowels. But to their astonishment that didn't happen. The bull heaved and shook with all its might, but Pickett held on. The bull raced around the arena, dragging Pickett and slamming him against the walls, but Pickett stuck like glue. He tried and tried to shake Pickett off. He kneeled and tried to rake Pickett off, but he couldn't reach the cowboy with his hoofs.

A tense hush fell upon the arena when the bull stood still and stopped moving its head. The crowd realized to its utter amazement that the bull was tiring from the weight and pressure the cowboy was applying to its neck. Suddenly Pickett leaped between Frijoli Chiquita's horns, wrapped his arms around the animal and squeezed with all his might. At the same time he pressed his knees against the bull's nostrils to cut off its breathing. He began to sway from side to side, and the crowd could see the bull starting to totter. Pickett was literally rocking Frijoli Chiquita to sleep.

That was too much for the amazed Mexicans. They let out agonized shrieks of anger and disbelief and began to hurl things into the bullring—cushions, bottles, knives, sticks, stones, shoes, whatever they had that they could throw. Pickett smiled up at the malevolent throng, ignoring the hail of missiles, answering their curses with his self-satisfied grin. A brick grazed Pickett's forehead, causing a trickle of blood down his cheek. But he held on, knowing in just a few more seconds the bull would collapse. He felt he had already been attached to the animal long enough to win the bet. Any second the bell should ring to declare him the victor. He could then go and see about Spradley.

A pain in his side more excruciating than any other he could remember sent shock waves throughout Pickett's body, and he believed for a second that he had been shot. Someone had thrown a full quart bottle of beer that cracked Pickett's ribs when it made impact. The intense pain caused Pickett to relax his stranglehold, and that was all the respite Frijoli Chiquita needed. He flung his head wildly trying to rid himself of his human burden.

In desperation, Pickett grabbed the horns again, but he had been weakened by the hit with the bottle of beer. Frijoli Chiquita raced around the bullring, dragging Pickett, slinging him around like a puppet, and banging him against the walls. The crowd was on its twenty-five thousand pairs of feet cheering wildly, anticipating that in an instant Pickett would be tossed to the ground and gored repeatedly.

During all this Miller had been screaming at the timekeeper to ring the bell. When he wouldn't, Miller told a cowboy named Vester Peg to take off his red shirt and run out and distract the bull the instant Pickett let go, and he instructed other cowboys to rope the bull's legs.

Pickett could see no way of getting away from the bull if he turned loose. But the strength was gone from his hands, and the pain in his side had become unbearable. He felt his fingers go numb, and he knew it was the end. A crescendo of joy rose from the crowd as the cowboy fell to the dust. Pickett stared into the fiery eyes of the bull as it charged, head lowered, horns aimed at his groin. He consigned his soul to God and waited for the impact. But the hit never came. The beast's belly brushed his nose as it passed over him. He scrambled to his feet and raced to the barrier, clutching his wounded side. Out of the corner of his eye, Pickett glimpsed Frijoli Chiquita chasing a cowboy waving a red cloth.

Having made it to safety, Pickett's first thought was for Spradley. He found the horse lying on its left side with two gaping holes in his right rump oozing blood. He just knew he'd have to put Spradley down, and he didn't have the heart to do it. Then an old Mexican, known simply as Jose, who had hired on with the show, said he could cure Spradley. He sent for some bananas and cursed a blue streak when yellow ones were delivered to him. He needed red ones. When Jose got the right fruit, he peeled the bananas and inserted one in each of the gore holes in the horse's rump. In less than an hour Spradley was on his feet. The wounds healed completely in a few days.

Pickett's first thought was for Spradley. He found the horse lying on its left side with two gaping holes in his right rump oozing blood. He just knew he'd have to put Spradley down, and he didn't have the heart to do it.

Pickett had to go back into the bull-ring to salute President Diaz in order for Miller to collect on the bet. There was no doubt that Pickett had exceeded the time required to satisfy the terms of the wager. The timekeeper had apologized lamely for not ringing the bell, explaining that his watch had stuck.

When Pickett reappeared, the stunned, angry crowd ran amok. The 101 cowboys feared they would be lynched and asked Miller for permission to load their carbines and pistols with real bullets instead of blanks and shoot their way out. But Miller said that would be suicidal. President Diaz finally ordered a company of *rurales* to provide safe conduct for the Miller crew. They used the broadsides of their swords and fired over the heads of the crowd. Milt Hinkle, a 101 cowboy at the time who would later become a famous bulldogger himself, described the escape:

> The captain (of the *rurales*) told Joe to get his people all in a bunch, and when we were all there, the *rurales* formed a ring around us with aimed rifles pointed at the maddened gang. The Americans and even Mexican Joe, one of our best ropers, were fighting mad. They called the Mexicans every name they knew, and they knew plenty. Fortunately very few of the Mexicans understood English, so we got some self-satisfaction.
>
> I had always felt kindly toward Mexicans before, but not at that moment. I couldn't understand any human being who could not find some admiration for the remarkable display of sheer courage such as Bill Pickett and his great horse Spradley had shown.
>
> They certainly were not good sportsmen. They seem to be unacquainted with fair play toward another man who was as good and brave as the Dusky Demon, Bill Pickett. But I tried to excuse those heels because I sort of understood their love for bullfighting.

Things had actually worked out for the best for Diaz and the Mexican government. They had allowed the contest to go on without literally breaking their word to prominent Americans. Pickett had not been killed, so there should be no diplomatic backlash. Still, the episode caused a lot of cross-border ill feelings for several years.

The show had to be guarded by the *rurales* for the remainder of its stay in Mexico. When the 101 crew crossed the Rio Grande, Miller, ever the opportunistic promoter, used the episode to drum up audiences for homecoming shows in San Antonio and Fort Worth. Pickett's fame spread far and wide. In Texas, his reputation rivaled that of another black native Texan, Jack Johnson, of Galveston, who had won the world heavyweight boxing championship in Australia less than a week after Pickett's bullring bout in Mexico.

Joe Miller's ballyhooing of Pickett's daredevil feat in Mexico City showed the same kind of insensitivity to Mexican culture that had led to the near tragic episode. If Miller had given serious consideration to the feelings of the Mexicans about their national sport, he would not have pressed the matter. After all, he was in their country. Why not just let them boast. Moreover the Mexicans had long-standing grievances against the North Americans because of cross-border cattle rustling and the frequent border violations by the United States Cavalry in pursuit of Apache and Kikapoo Indians. Those incursions were made mostly by black buffalo soldiers of the famed Ninth Cavalry Regiment.

The Diaz government also harbored suspicions that North Americans were abetting rebelling elements seeking to overthrow the regime. Those suspicions became evident when the show first crossed the border and was subjected to intense searches for contraband weapons. Everything and everybody were searched. Colonel Zack Miller later recounted that the hoochy-koochy dancers in the sideshow were "almost stripped searched." That, of course, may have had little to do with weapons.

Of course, the 101 folks did not set out intentionally to offend the Mexicans. Indeed, they felt quite put-upon from the outset, what with the searches, the thefts of show property, and the constant efforts of the Mexicans to cheat them. They saw the poverty around them, but that did not excuse the stealing.

Then there was the parade incident. A crowd attacked the Indians in the show—who for the most part were Poncas—thinking they were Apaches. The *rurales* had to save the Indians from a massacre.

Historically, although the cowboys probably didn't know it, they had some justification for feeling that the Mexicans were poor sports. Bullfighters had been treated quite different-ly when they were imported to Dodge City in 1884 for that city's Fourth of July celebration. The bullfighters put on daz-zling displays of grace and courage, but the crowd really didn't appreciate the finer points of bullfighting. They called out to one matador to "throw him," as his bull charged past. Obligingly the bullfighter tried and was almost killed in the process. The crowd cheered the bullfighter for his effort, and then gave him an even bigger ovation when he finished the bull in the traditional way.

Minor details of the Mexico City episode have varied in different retellings. As Zack Miller recalled it years later, for example, Pickett selected Frijoli Chiquita at the corral. There was no mention of Bonito. Miller was an old man at the time. In *Buckskin and Spurs*, Glenn Shirley has the bull gore Spradley in the shoulder. Shirley also has Pickett knocked loose from the bull by a brick instead of a bottle of beer. But in all fundamental respects, all the stories jibe. All say Spradley was cured with the red bananas.

Pickett did not perform in San Antonio and Fort Worth. He was still nursing his wounds. Nevertheless, the show's publicity played up the Mexico City episode grandly. When the show hit Fort Worth on January 3, 1909, the *Fort Worth Telegram* ran a picture from the Mexican newspaper *El Imparcial* showing Pickett between the bull's horns with a stranglehold on the animal's neck, while the air is filled with cushions and other missiles. The caption to the picture said: "This remarkable photograph from *El Imparcial* shows the enraged bull trying to shake the Negro off. Cushions and other missiles are being hurled at him by the enraged Mexicans."

A story accompanying the picture was headlined: "Texas Negro Fights Big Bull Unarmed In Mexican Ring."

The text of the story read:

William Pickett, a strapping Negro, whose home is in Taylor, Texas, member of the Miller Brothers 101 Ranch Wild West Show, gave hand-to-horns battle to a bull in the Mexico City ring on Wednesday, a week ago, receiving injuries from which he is still suffering.

Twenty-five thousand persons, the largest crowd in the history of the great El Toro amphitheater, saw the performance. Most of them went armed with missiles for the man who dared to show his contempt for their beloved toreadors' exhibitions. They pelted him with opened knives, bottles, stones, oranges, and cushions as he struggled with the animal.

91

Toro! Toro! Toro!: Dance with a Killer Bull

Pickett remained in the arena for fifteen minutes, as Mr. Miller (Joe) had wagered $1,000 he would do. He did not throw the bull to the ground, for a bottle hit him in the side.

The bull was provided by the Tepeyahualco ganderia, famed for the fierceness of its stock. Pickett was accompanied in the arena by four other mounted cowboys. The bull came in with a snort and a rush and never ceased attacking the horses from the moment he entered.

The Negro at once found himself at a disadvantage, for, in his usual performances the men are able to chase a steer so that Pickett can ride up. He tried several times to get the bull in the right position, but the cowboys had all they could do to protect their horses by firing blank cartridges in the face of the bull. Pickett made an attempt from an awkward position and failed to get hold. He narrowly escaped and rode out of the ring to jeers and howls.

He entered again and rode straight at the wildly charging bull and caught it by the horns, but they were wet with the blood of his horse, and he could not hold them.

Three attempts won more howls and missiles of all kinds. Finally, Pickett flung himself between the bulls' horns. He caught the bull and, tossed from right and left, managed to fasten his hold. The bull stopped, puzzled. Then the bottle was thrown and Pickett turned loose his hold and staggered back. The bull rushed to gore the Negro, but ran over his body without inflicting a serious wound. As the bull turned to attack again, the bullfighters led the infuriated animal away with their capes.

Again, there are minor variations in the story. But the essential facts are the same. The episode would become a staple of 101 publicity for years to come until the show folded its tents and stole away into the dusty pages of history.

Chapter Eight

....

Big House on the Prairie

B ILL PICKETT'S PRESENCE GAVE THE 101 RANCH
Wild West Show something special that no similar show
could boast. So did his absence. Pickett was absent from
the show for most of its 1909 tour, but the audiences in
many of the cities and towns the show played didn't know he
wasn't going to perform until they'd already paid their admission and seen the show. Few complained because it was a very
good show, even without its star attraction.

From January until September, Pickett stayed in Oklahoma
recovering from the cuts, scrapes, and cracked bones he had
suffered in his close-to-fatal encounter with Frijoli Chiquita.
Nevertheless, the Miller brothers could not resist capitalizing
upon the tremendous publicity that reverberated from that
extraordinary effort. Pickett was the only performer named in
newspaper ads, and the programs always included hyperbolic
references to Pickett's Mexico City exploit. The impression

was often given that there would be a reenactment of that episode during the show.

Different cowboys handled the bulldogging in Pickett's absence, but they did it less spectacularly. No biting was attempted. But even without Pickett's special touch, bulldogging was a thrilling and dangerous act. Two of the substitutes were injured seriously. One almost died from being gored.

Pickett was smart enough to know that he would never break through the walls of prejudice that kept most blacks out of cowboy competitions and exhibitions, unless he came up with something new.

The use of Pickett's name in the show's publicity—even when he was not on the tour—underscored his importance to the show, and led the authors of The Negro Cowboys, Phillip Dunham and Everett L. Jones, to suggest that without him the 101 Ranch story would have been "just another Wild West yarn." There is some truth in that assessment, but the proposition cuts both ways. It is doubtful that Pickett, without the resources of the 101, could have climbed to the level of stardom he eventually achieved. Granted, he had done well prior to hooking up with the Millers, which was remarkable at a time when there was so much prejudice against blacks.

Pickett had come a long way from his obscure beginnings in Travis County, Texas, when he met the Millers. He had been able to do so because of his grit, his athletic ability, and his intelligence. Pickett was smart enough to know that he would never break through the walls of prejudice that kept most blacks out of cowboy competitions and exhibitions, unless he came up with something new. He could ride and rope and break horses with the best of them. But he knew he would never be allowed to be a star attraction or even be permitted to compete in many roundups if he just did what other cowboys did. So he concentrated on doing something unique, something people would pay to see regardless of the color of the man performing.

Still Pickett had gone about as far as he could go. To go farther he needed the Millers and their traveling show, which was one of the biggest and best of all the Wild West shows.

The immense wealth generated by the multifaceted Miller ranch paid the freight for the roving spectacular in which Pickett was the brightest star. That wealth steadily grew, despite the excesses of the Miller brothers' venture into show business. Much of that was due to George Miller's financial expertise. George invested in the oil industry and made a killing. The ranch had its own refinery. Joe Miller's agricultural pursuits paid off well. Zack Miller was a remarkable trader in cattle, horses, and mules. Their talents meshed almost perfectly.

In 1909, the ranch had prospered so much that the family was hardly fazed by a major catastrophe that occurred shortly after the show returned from Mexico. On January 14, 1909, the Miller mansion burned to the ground with all its contents and furnishings. The mansion had been one of the most luxurious and richly appointed in Oklahoma, but it was insured for only $7,500. Rebuilding commenced immediately, and out of the cinders of the palatial mansion built to memorialize G. W. Miller, the founder of the ranch, the famous "White House" arose.

The three-story colonial mansion, the center and symbol of the Millers' empire, would welcome dignitaries from all walks of life and from around the nation and the world in the years to come. Because of Pickett's star status, his kids would have free run of the house whenever they were at the ranch.

On January 14, 1909, the Miller mansion burned to the ground with all its contents and furnishings. The mansion had been one of the most luxurious and richly appointed in Oklahoma, but it was insured for only $7,500.

To prevent the possibility of its suffering the same fate as its predecessor, the new mansion was built almost entirely of steel and concrete. For its day it had every modern convenience, including electric lights, steam heat, hot and cold running water, and a rudimentary form of air-conditioning. Each of the nine bedrooms on the second floor of the White House had its own bathroom, a living room, and a vestibule. No walls divided the third floor. It was one huge open bay, big enough for dancing or to install fifty four-poster beds for visitors during rodeo season. Pictures of livestock and buffaloes adorned the walls. Guests could stroll out on a screened balcony to observe the panorama of the ranch. A library, a dining room, the kitchen, and the den occupied the first floor.

Simultaneously with the construction of the White House, the Millers were putting together the 1909 show, which hit the road in April of that year, embarking again from Ponca City with great fanfare. The show toured Oklahoma for a month before invading Missouri and moving on through Indiana, Ohio, and Pennsylvania. Throughout its journey, the show capitalized on the man who was not there.

"Pickett Dusky Demon of Oklahoma reproducing the fight for life in a Mexican bull ring. Only man in human history who ever battled barehanded with a Spanish bull and escaped alive," screamed the show's broadsheets.

Pickett rejoined the show in September in Wichita Falls, Texas. His nine-month recuperation had been the longest ever for a man who customarily performed hurt. In 1905 in Hot Springs, Arkansas, for example, Pickett had bulldogged steers daily with his arm in a sling. He finished the 1909 season without further serious injury.

Before the 1910 tour commenced, Pickett moved his family into a spacious house near the 101 Ranch a few miles from the White House. There is some dispute as to whether Pickett owned the property or was just allowed to use it. Pickett descendants say he owned it and insist that he could afford it. They say the Millers paid him more money on the side than the standard wages for a top cowhand. Whatever the case, the Picketts had their own relatively big house on the prairie when the show opened in St. Louis on April 16, 1910.

The next three seasons went exceedingly well, both for the Millers and for Pickett. In between seasons Pickett and most of the other cowboys returned to work to prepare horses and steers for the next tour. During all those years, Pickett was the star attraction, the only cowboy listed on the program by name, although he was traveling in some fast company that included fellow performers who would go on to become world champions in professional rodeo events. Among them were Milt Hinkle, Clarence Shultz, Chester Byers, Hank Durnell, Montana Jack Ray, Tom Eckhardt, Buck Steven, Blanch McGaughy, and Lulu Parr.

During the years 1910 through 1913, the show adhered to basically the same format A. K. Greenland rhapsodized effusively about in an August 15, 1911, article in *Billboard*. The show was booked into the Boston Arena; however, Greenland began his account with the parade on the Boston Commons.

> We heard a trumpet, then a band. The pageant advances, led by the pick of Boston's police department. Next comes a set of lusty ranchmen, characteristically straddling impetuous bronchos. A long train of Indians, bedecked in feathers and brilliant war paint, now jog before us. Another cowboy, then a train of big, heavy show wagons, the cowgirls, gracefully mounted, joyously greet you. Forthwith you begin to picture the West (as a) land of dream and enchantment. The East and historic New England assume a far less superior station in your opinion. Here come the Mexicans, preceded by "Dusky" Bill Pickett. Following them comes the huge, large horned bull, carrying a human load on its back with the most perfect docility. There are the Cossacks, the buffalo, more cowboys and cowgirls, brought to a close by the piping calliope.

Greenland tells of his party being greeted by the Miller brothers, Joe, Zack, and George, and being shown their seats by
George Arlington. He describes the 550-by-390-foot arena
tent, the special tent for the horses, and the cook tent. And he
points out that there are eleven hundred persons associated
with the show and six hundred animals, among which are elephants, camels, horses, buffaloes, long-horned steers, oxens,
mules, and ponies.

The band plays an overture; Joe Miller gives a salutatory
speech, tells the directors to let the performers pass in review.
That done, the individual acts begin. Greenland refers to them
as "displays," but act is a more appropriate term. The ensemble
presentation was the first act.

Act Two featured a dash through the arena of mounted
performers that included "cowboys from headquarters; Sioux
Indians from Pine Ridge; cowboys from Cowskin Camp; a
band of Cheyenne redskins from Oklahoma; cowboys from
Horse Shoe Bend; Snake Indians from the Creek reservation; a
troupe of Russian Imperial Cossacks, followed by Lucca, their
prince; a collection of Mexican *vaqueros* and *rurales*; cowgirls;
Chief Eagle Feather of the Sioux; Pickett, the Dusky Demon;
D. V. Tantlinger, chief of the cowboys; and lastly and therefore
most important, Joseph P. Miller."

Act Three depicted the Pony Express with an armed cowboy racing around the arena with a pouch over his shoulder.
Act Four was a demonstration of prowess with ropes in which
running horses were lassoed and a rope artist spun elaborate

figures and jumped through loops. Act Five was an enactment of a stagecoach robbery by some Mexican bandits, who are sur- prised and vanquished by cowboys and *rurales* after much shooting and feigning of injuries.

Greenland skipped Act Six and went on to write: "Display No. 7 calls our attention to Pickett, the modern Ursus in a demonstration of courage, nerve, strength and agility in which he duplicates his feat of conquering a Spanish bull unarmed and unaided, by forcing the largest of bulls to the tanbark of sheer strength." The Ursus reference was an allusion to the popular novel *Quo Vadis*. (In the movie of the same name, Ursus is the giant who saves Deborah Kerr, who is chained to a stake in the arena of the Roman Coliseum, from a charging Spanish bull by taking on the bull barehanded and breaking its neck.) Pickett did not duplicate his Mexico City exploit, and the steers he bulldogged may have had Spanish blood, but not the fighting kind. Like most of the show's spectators, Greenland was so excited by Pickett's bulldogging act that he did not quibble over small details.

Act Nine presented Tantlinger throwing his boomerang and showing how it could be used for hunting or fighting. Act Ten was a combination, intricate quadrille on horseback and Edith Tantlinger's demonstration of her expertise with a shot- gun. Act Twelve was an exhibition of equine high stepping and jumping. Act Thirteen portrayed a horse thief, stealing a horse, fleeing with it, getting captured, and "subsequent treat- ment accorded any such miscreant."

Act Fourteen was an exhibition of military riding tactics that concluded with a three-horse Roman standing mount. Act Fifteen was the 101's answer to Annie Oakley in rifle shooting, Princess Wenona. Act Sixteen was a game of football on horseback. Acts Seventeen and Eighteen were trick riding. In Act Nineteen, a cowboy rode a bucking buffalo without a bridle. Act Twenty was an indoor version of the attack on the wagon train that almost caused a panic at the Editorial Association convention in 1905.

Pickett's act frequently was shifted to different spots in the show. In his version of a typical 101 show in a 1969 magazine article, Milt Hinkle placed Pickett in the twentieth act: "No. 20. Steer wrestling by Bill Pickett, the Dusky Demon and the first steer wrestler; and Milt Hinkle, the first white man to do Pickett's stunt, plus Tom Eckhard, Ed Lindsey and Lafe Lewman."

During 1912 alone, Pickett traveled more than seventeen thousand miles through twenty-two states and three Canadian provinces with the 101 show. He put on more than four hundred performances. The show had its share of unpredictable problems during that season, including a fire among the packed tents near Milwaukee in early August. The train was halted near a creek, and Pickett was pressed into a bucket brigade to put out the fire. A week later, near Lancaster, Wisconsin, the train hit a split rail, demolishing four cars, killing ten horses and injuring thirty more. But the show weathered those storms and wound up that year well in the black and in good shape for its 1913 tour.

Pickett departed from the successful 1913 tour before the season ended, but it wasn't because of an injury. He had to strike out for New York in late October to catch a ship that would take him farther away from the two big houses on the prairie than he'd ever been or ever dreamed of going.

Chapter Nine

Don't Cry for Me, Argentina

OTHING FRIJOLI CHIQUITA COULD HAVE DONE
to Bill Pickett's stomach with his long, sharp horns could
have felt worse than what the famous bulldogger experienced two weeks after he embarked from Brooklyn, New
York, on November 1, 1913, bound for Buenos Aires,
Argentina. At least that's what Pickett thought at the time.
The Atlantic Ocean had thrown a conniption. The
Caribbean was bucking like a wild mustang trying to pitch a
cowboy off its back. The cowboy in this case was the ship.
Every time the sea tossed it up and down and rolled it from
side to side, something inside Pickett's stomach imitated those
motions and made him bring up everything he'd eaten. It was
worse if he hadn't eaten. Most of the other performers had
never been on a ship either, and they were having the same
problem. The crew of the *Varsara* kept telling the landlubbers
to eat a lot to keep from being seasick. No one wanted to eat

under the circumstances. The very thought of food made Pickett nauseous. But he forced himself to eat in order to have something to toss up besides his guts.

He'd heard they had two more weeks on that bucking ocean before they reached Argentina, and he seriously doubted he'd make it. The very thought of being out of sight of land that much longer was disquieting. The rough seas made matters worse, and the fact that he had lots of company in that misery didn't help. He thought of the story of Jonah falling overboard and being swallowed by a whale. That didn't bother him. His problem was that he felt like he'd swallowed a whale.

He thought of the story of Jonah falling overboard and being swallowed by a whale. That didn't bother him. His problem was that he felt like he'd swallowed a whale.

Pickett cursed the minute he'd agreed to make the South American tour. That was Edward Arlington's idea, and it only involved a few select performers from the 101 show and the Buffalo Bill show. In addition to Pickett, the cast included Milt Hinkle, Otto Kline, Mabel Kline, Hank Durnell, Bob Anderson, Lulu Parr, Jane Fuller, Charlie Aldridge, Billy Lorette, Beau Brousseau, and world champion trick roper Chester Byers. Byers had made a previous South American tour with XIT Ranch Wild West Show in 1910. He got seasick, too.

Like the blindness that came and went mysteriously more than twenty years before, Pickett's seasickness left just before the ship docked off the coast of Brazil to take on water and other supplies. His brain and stomach had adjusted to the pitch and roll of the sea by the time the ship struck out again for Buenos Aires. Trouble, however, was not over yet for *Varsara* and its crew of Wild West performers. Pickett thought at first that the four Indians they sewed up in canvas bags and pitched into the sea had succumbed to seasickness. He became worried, however, when he found out that they had smallpox. The contagion, however, was contained for the most part in the steerage where the Indians were billeted. Pickett rode in first class with the other top performers. Hank Durnell, however, did get it. He pleaded to be pitched overboard. His request was denied, and Durnell survived.

Winter had been setting in when the ship left Brooklyn. It was summer when the trouble-plagued *Varsara* docked in Buenos Aires, which seemed, after the long voyage, like the most beautiful place Pickett had ever seen. It was Oklahoma, Texas, Arizona, Missouri, and Arkansas all rolled into one. It was land, firm ground that did not move when you moved. Pickett never dreamed he'd be as overjoyed to see any place as he was to feast his eyes on Buenos Aires, Argentina.

How much Edward Arlington paid the port officials to keep the ship from being quarantined because of the smallpox outbreak, Pickett didn't know and didn't care. In any event, the Indians covered their heads and faces with their blankets and the health inspectors cleared them. Arlington could not, however, get the horses past the livestock inspectors. All of the horses had to be killed and burned when Otto Kline's trick riding horse was found to have the highly infectious disease glanders. Pickett was overjoyed that he had left Spradley behind with the 101 show. That little spraddle-legged bay pony led a charmed life. Everyone was ready to put him down at the 101 when he picked up that splinter jumping a rail and the wound turned into a tumor. Pickett had operated on Spradley himself and nursed him back to health. Then there was the goring by that vicious bull Chiquita Frijoli in Mexico City. Pickett still had not figured out what was in those red bananas that healed Spradley's wounds, but he'd be forever grateful to old Pedro for knowing about them. He had decided not to take Spradley to South America at the last minute for no particular reason.

. . . Edward Arlington paid the port officials to keep the ship from being quarantined because of the smallpox outbreak. . .

For the show, Arlington bought two dozen saddle horses, ten bucking horses, four steers to ride and three steers for Pickett and Hinkle to bulldog. The show was held at the Park of the Japanese. Hinkle made this comment about the opening of the show:

> We opened on Sunday and had a big crowd. Bill Pickett and I had a lot of fun bulldogging the "green" steers and we went over in a big way with the audience. We gave three shows that day, with full houses. The newspaper gave us lots of good publicity in the next morning's issue, so the show was making money.

When Hinkle referred to the steers as being green, he meant they'd never been wrestled down before. The virgin Argentine steers ran faster, kicked harder, and did everything in their power to avoid being thrown. The challenges they presented to the bulldoggers made their act all the more thrilling to the crowds that packed the house. The audiences, of course, also were green. They'd never seen any bulldogging at all, much less Pickett's bite 'em style. The XIT Ranch had taken a show there two years earlier, but it had no bulldoggers.

Pickett had for the most part given up performing his trademark stunt in the United States because of all the stink created by the humane societies, but he faced no such restrictions in Argentina. The crowds responded to it with great gusto.

One evening Hinkle informed Edward Arlington that he had been invited by a big rancher to spend some time on his ranch in the Pampas. Arlington told Hinkle he could not leave the show for any reason at any time.

"You and Bill Pickett are the only bulldoggers we have and that is our feature act," said Arlington.

Hinkle did go, however, and left Pickett to do all of the bulldogging for the remainder of the stay in Buenos Aires. Before he left, Hinkle substituted in another show in Buenos Aires for an alligator wrestler who had suffered the misfortune of getting his arm bitten off. Hinkle escaped that feat with both arms. Despite their continuing friendly rivalry, Pickett declined to wrestle an alligator.

With Hinkle gone, it fell to Pickett to keep the crowds satisfied. His was the act they primarily came to see, and the Dusky Demon gave it his best effort. He reached into his bag of tricks for crowd-pleasing gimmicks. He had his hands tied behind his back sometimes before throwing the steers with his teeth. He put an arm in a sling sometimes, although he had no injury. And he frequently repeated the stunt that always brought the crowds to their feet, i.e., throwing a particularly combative steer twice. The Argentineans didn't know what Pickett would do next, and they kept coming to the Park of the Japanese to find out. Pickett never found out why they called that place the Park of the Japanese. The whole time he was there he never saw any Japanese people. He saw Indians, Germans, Italians, Frenchmen, and a few black people, but no Japanese.

He had his hands tied behind his back sometimes before throwing the steers with his teeth. He put an arm in a sling sometimes, although he had no injury. And he frequently repeated . . . throwing a particularly combative steer twice. The Argentineans didn't know what Pickett would do next . . .

For his performances Pickett sometimes dressed like a gaucho, much to the delight of the spectators. He didn't go in for costumes much. Guy Weadick once persuaded him to dress up like a Spanish bullfighter. But he felt silly. He was a showman, but he was no clown. The gaucho outfit, although showy, was the ordinary garb of those Argentine cowboys. Pickett felt a kinship with the gauchos because they were so much like American cowboys, and like him, they were part Indian.

Except for the language, Argentina was very much like the United States. Because he'd spent so much time in Mexico and worked around Mexicans so much, Pickett didn't have

Hall of Fame cowboy Bill Pickett.

Photo courtesy of North Fort Worth Historical Society

A young Bill Pickett.

Photo courtesy of Frank S. Phillips and Gilbert Pittman

Frank S. Phillips, Pickett's great-grandson, crouches next to
Pickett's grave near the 101 Ranch in Oklahoma.

Photo courtesy of Frank S. Phillips

The two sets of the "Legends of the West" stamp series, with the "incorrect" Pickett stamp included in the top set and the corrected version in the lower set. In both sets, the Pickett stamp is located in the second row from the top, second from the left. The "incorrect" Pickett pictured actually is Ben Pickett, Bill's brother.

A closer look at the two stamps.

Bill Pickett applies his patented "lip-bite" to a steer.

Photo courtesy of North Fort Worth Historical Society

Pickett hits the dirt, taking the steer with him.

Photo courtesy of North Fort Worth Historical Society

Statue of Bill Pickett in a classic steer-wrestling move.
Photo courtesy of North Fort Worth Historical Society

much of a problem with the language. Their Spanish was a little different from the Spanish in Mexico, but after a little while he got used to it. The food was good there too, especially the beef. He liked to go to some of the sidewalk restaurants where they broiled the meat over open spits. Also, they had good beer and prime cigars. In Buenos Aires he felt at ease and unthreatened wherever he went. It wasn't like the United States, where he was treated like royalty on the ranch or when he was on the show grounds but was often insulted or mistreated because of his race in other places.

While Pickett was keeping the crowds satisfied in Buenos Aires, Hinkle was wandering around the Pampas and all the way up to Paraguay and Bolivia, participating in rodeos, fighting bandits and Indians, herding cattle, and seriously entertaining the idea of becoming an Argentinean rancher. Then circumstances brought him back from the South American boondocks. He found a cablegram from Zack Miller that said: "I want you to answer my letters and I want you to meet me in New York on April 1. Going to London. Must have you and Pickett."

The 101 performers Arlington had taken to Argentina did not have time to go back to the ranch. They had to do a two-week stint in Madison Square Garden before making the Atlantic crossing to England. They headed straight for New York just as summer was turning into fall in Buenos Aires and winter was melting into spring in Manhattan. Pickett would always remember Argentina fondly. A journey that had started out with a severe case of seasickness had been transformed into a round-trip with traces of a new kind of homesickness.

It was during that 1914 stand in Madison Square Garden that, according to one account, the steer got away and Pickett had to drag it out of the grandstand. A big green steer came out of the chute and built up momentum so quickly that they couldn't catch him. The steer bolted up the ramp into the grandstand and dragged a cowboy named Billy Binder along with him. Pickett rode his horse up the steps and piled onto the steer. The two of them dragged the spooked animal back into the arena. That account, of course, is not nearly as hair-raising as the one featuring Pickett and Rogers, which is why all the other stories about Pickett cite the Zack Miller version of the story. Assuming that the Bailey Hanes version is at least the second retrieval of a headstrong steer from the grandstand in Madison Square Garden, the incident provided a fitting send-off for the 101 show's voyage to England.

Chapter Ten
....

A Little Bit of England

WHEN THE BIG BRIGHT YELLOW MERCEDES
sped off with Bill Pickett in the backseat, some of the
performers who saw the pickup were awestruck. The
thought occurred to them that good old Bill Pickett,
the proper, ever-faithful family man, who had never been
known to fool around, had been corrupted by London. Perhaps
he'd taken on the ways of the roper-rider George Hooker.

In London, Hooker, ever the amorous opportunist, had
been taken in tow by a wealthy society lady, who picked him
up every evening in a big black Mercedes and brought him
back the next day at show time. Hooker, who was part black,
part Mexican, was a strikingly handsome man. Wherever he
went he managed to attract female companionship. Many of
the racially prejudiced cowboys and show hands were morally
offended by Hooker's affair with the wealthy Englishwoman.
According to Zack Miller, some of them had conspired "to fix

George up for slow traveling if they ever caught him bragging about bedding up with a white woman." Hooker didn't boast, although the affair continued throughout the show's stay in England. When the show left, Miller said, "He (Hooker) was wearing a finger ring with a diamond that gathered light like the sun."

The yellow limousine that picked up Bill Pickett, however, did not belong to any adventuresome English lady. It was the property of Hugh Cecil Lowther, fifth earl of Lonsdale, also known as "The Yellow Earl" and called by a few friends "Lordy." His Lordship was known as the Yellow Earl because all his cars and carriages were of that brilliant hue. In royal processions, Lonsdale's yellow entourage eclipsed that of the king and queen. He lived lavishly and flamboyantly at the end of the prim and proper Victorian era and the dawn of the Edwardian period. His scandalous and extravagant behavior made him popular with the British public and something of an embarrassment to the crown. His dalliances with various women, most notably the famous actress Lily Langtry, provided ample grist for the gossip mills.

He lived lavishly and flamboyantly at the end of the prim and proper Victorian era and the dawn of the Edwardian period. His scandalous and extravagant behavior made him popular with the British public and something of an embarrassment to the crown.

The earl of Lonsdale also had a passionate interest in sports, primarily boxing, hunting, and equestrian events. The 101 was, in a phrase, the earl's "cup of tea," and he took a particular fancy to Pickett's bulldogging act. That's why he had invited the bulldogger to his country estate to dine.

Zack Miller was mistaken in asserting that the earl had invited Pickett to dinner so his children could see close-up a man who could throw a steer. Lonsdale had no children, at least no legitimate ones. His wife couldn't have children because of injuries she suffered in a riding accident. He had one illegitimate child by opera singer Violet Cameron, one of the great stage beauties of the period. That child would have been in its twenties by the time the 101 show hit England in 1914. It was the earl, himself, who wanted the benefit of Pickett's company, simply because he appreciated fine athletes.

Lonsdale's reputation as a sportsman and a gentleman who valued fair play was borne out by an incident involving another famous American athlete that occurred while the 101 show was playing London. When Jack Johnson, then in exile but still the undefeated world's heavyweight boxing champion, was mugged and robbed in London, it was the earl of Lonsdale he sought out for help.

On his way to Lowther Castle, Pickett was refreshed by the greenery of the rolling English countryside. The color and texture were different from Texas, but the English landscape reminded him in some respects of the Texas hill country. It really was good to get out of the crush and the noise of the city for a little while.

Pickett was not prepared, however, for the grandeur of Lowther Castle. By his estimate it was four times as big as the White House at 101 Ranch, and it was straight out of some of those stories about armored knights and princesses that his girls read to him when he was blind. He was even less prepared for the banquet room, where the eight-course meal was served. It looked to him to be about half the size of the barn at the 101 Ranch.

Although the number and variety of the eating tools confused him a bit, Pickett observed what the others did and improvised his way through all eight courses without embarrassing himself. But he was mightily impressed. Here he was, this black cowboy from Taylor, Texas, with a fifth-grade education, sitting elbow to elbow with rich, sophisticated people around a table as long as the 101 dining room, being served by uniformed white waiters who wouldn't let his glass stay empty. It was heady stuff. He was, so to speak, picking in high cotton.

Although the number and variety of the eating tools confused him a bit, Pickett observed what the others did and improvised his way through all eight courses . . .

Pickett was not impressed very much by champagne. It struck him as being little more than expensive soda pop. He supposed that the bear at the ranch would love it. The bear was kept just outside the souvenir shop. It constantly begged visitors for soda pop. It drank so much of the stuff that it ballooned into a bloated giant. One thing about the champagne, though, Pickett discovered; it helped conversation when one drank enough of it.

When the men and women separated after dinner, Pickett told stories of his adventures in bulldogging, particularly about the Mexico City episode. During that time, they drank brandy and smoked cigars. Pickett loved a good cigar, and those provided by the earl were the best tasting and smoothest smoking he'd ever lit up.

Pickett explained his bite 'em style, and everyone was intrigued. But all agreed that it couldn't be done in England because of the humane societies. Pickett pointed out that for the same reason he had to discontinue using that technique in the United States.

One gentleman remarked that Pickett was not a very big man and marveled at his ability to throw a steer bare-handed. Pickett gave him the same response to that strength question that he'd given to a Phoenix, Arizona, reporter ten years earlier:

"I can lift a two-hundred-pound bag of salt over my head with one movement. People tell me that's pretty strong."

Another gentleman scrupulously pointed out that what Pickett had been doing when he was biting steers should not have been called bulldogging.

"In the old British sport of bull baiting the dogs bit the bulls in the lower lip. They could do that, because unlike you, the bulldogs have flat noses. You sir, were biting the steers in the upper lip or nose," he said.

Pickett conceded the point, and everyone else agreed that the nose was close enough. The dinner guests grew slack-jawed when Pickett went into detail about the Mexico City episode.

They simply could not believe anyone could have the "how do you say . . . guts" to do such a thing.

One of the guests expressed doubts that Pickett could bulldog a wild Highland steer. Pickett said he'd already dropped one the day before.

When the bulldogger returned from his day with the British gentry, Zack Miller asked how it went. Pickett gave Miller a song and dance about having trouble with the cutlery and the champagne and how busy he was trying to keep up with the fast-moving courses. He knew that was what Miller wanted to hear. Pickett thought it polite to not let on about how much he had really enjoyed his outing and being treated as an equal in upper-class British society.

Miller told Pickett to go to the mess tent and get them to fix him something to eat if he was still hungry. Pickett did that because, in fact, he was hungry again after the long drive back from the country in the big yellow Mercedes.

The 101 Ranch Wild West Show had come to England at the invitation of the British government. Some behind-the-scenes prodding by Sir Thomas Lipton, the tea potentate, played a role in that. Zack Miller had met Lipton in 1911 when the show was filming a movie in Santa Monica Canyon in Venus, California. The show was in winter quarters there at the time, and all of its cowboys, Indians, cattle, stagecoaches, horses, and buffalo were rented out to producer-director Thomas Ince for $2,500 a week. It was there in what came to be called "Inceville" that the movies *War on the Plains*, *Battle of the Red Men, The Indian Massacre,* and *The Lieutenant's Last Fall* were made. The hospitality extended to Lipton during the filming was recompensed three years later. Lipton exerted considerable influence to make it possible for the 101 show to follow the European trail blazed by Buffalo Bill. The show, which arrived in London on April 29, 1914, was part of the Anglo-American Exposition commemorating a century of peace between the two countries.

At a party on the evening of the show's arrival, the earl of Lonsdale told Zack Miller about a problem with a horse show he was managing at the time. He'd engaged five Cossack riders for the show, and they'd just informed him they couldn't make it. Miller loaned the earl five Cossack riders from the 101 show. That saved the day for the earl, and he returned the favor soon thereafter.

On Monday, May 25, 1914, the *London Times* took note of the opening of the 101 show in this manner:

> The first full review of the 101 Wild West in the remodeled stadium at the Anglo-American Exhibition took place Saturday ... This is the first time the Miller Brothers' cowboys and cowgirls, who come from the 101 Ranch at Bliss, Oklahoma, have performed out of America.

Either the *Times* considered Canada and Mexico part of America or Miller's press agents were selling the British public a bill of goods about their being the first persons outside the United States to be privileged to see the show.

The latter appears to have been the case, judging by this report in the *Daily Mirror* of May 27, 1914:

> Quite the most attractive feature of the Anglo-American Exposition at Shepherd's Bush is the performance which is being given twice daily in the Stadium by The 101 Ranch Real Wild West. This representation of life in the prairies is a wonderful spectacle and one which is wholly new to Londoners and every one of the performers was born and reared on the 101 Ranch, from which the show takes its name . . .
>
> This is the first time they have been out of America, and they only arrived in this country two weeks ago. . .

Pickett was a big hit, but he became more of a public fascination because of circumstances that had little to do with his skill and daring. The humane societies began picking on Pickett. They said his twisting a steer's neck to throw it amounted to cruelty to animals. Their picketing of Pickett created such a furor that Pickett was arrested for cruelty to dumb beasts. Miller paid the equivalent of twenty-five dollars to get his bulldogger out of jail. Miller then conceived the bright idea of simply paying the authorities twenty-five dollars a week throughout the show's stay in England. That way Pickett could continue bulldogging without being arrested.

And so it was. The humane societies screamed. Pickett bulldogged. Miller paid the police, and the continuing controversy kept the crowds flocking to the show. Miller speculated that he could have made a fortune if Pickett had still been bulldogging bite 'em style.

The earl of Lonsdale arranged with the Millers for a special performance for the Royal Family. Milt Hinkle took credit for helping Zack Miller select the acts for the show. Hinkle wrote:

> Zack and I got our heads together and lined up a program of the outstanding acts, plus a push Ball Game between the cowboys and Indians, with players riding horseback. Then there was trick roping by Sam Garrett and the Burns brothers, Fred and Ed. Then came the Cossack riding, followed by me riding Old Scarback and St. Louis, two real good bucking horses and, of course, Bill Pickett, to bulldog steers.

Both Miller and Hinkle insist that King George and his mother, Queen Mary, were there and that the king became so excited that he clapped his hands in a most unkingly manner and the queen had to remind him of the protocol.

> His Majesty and party sat in their royal boxes till the last stunt was pulled. In the meantime, the earl of Lonsdale sent word to line up the entire troupe at the gate when the show was over; that the royal party wanted to shake hands with each performer, which they did, bowing and smiling and saying over and over: "Most wonderful exhibition! Most wonderful exhibition!"

Once again Miller and Hinkle may have expanded the truth a bit. *The London Daily Chronicle* covered the event and made no mention of the king's being there in its June 26, 1914, edition. Here's part of that report:

> Queen Alexandra yesterday afternoon paid a visit to the Anglo-American Exhibition at Shepherd's-bush

(sic) for the primary purpose of witnessing the "Wild West" performance given within the Stadium. In four motor-cars her Majesty and the party by whom she was accompanied set out from Marlborough House shortly after three o'clock. In the first car were Queen Alexandra herself and the Empress Marie of Russia, attended by Sir Colin Keppel; in the second were the Princess Royal and her daughter, Princess Maud, together with the Hon. Violet Vivian; the third car accommodated the Countess of Antrim, Colonel Streatfield, Prince Chervachidze, and Countess Mengden; and seated in the fourth were General Sir Dighton Probyn and the Hon. Charlotte Knollys.

On arrival at the Stadium Queen Alexandra was received by the Earl of Lonsdale and Sir John Cockburn, by whom the distinguished party were escorted to the Royal tribune. To the right of her Majesty sat her sister, the Empress Marie, the Princess Royal, and Princess Maud; and immediately on the left of Queen Alexandra was seated Lord Lonsdale. With the greatest interest the Royal visitors followed every detail of the diversified, and some respects thrilling, program; and if one may judge by the emphatic approval which Queen Alexandra bestowed on various items, her Majesty thoroughly enjoyed the performance. More than that, Queen Alexandra took so many snapshots during the entertainment that her camera had to be replenished with a fresh spool of films; and before she left the Stadium she specially requested that the entire series of photos bearing on the performance should be forwarded to her in order to supplement her own collection. As the Royal party drove off, the members of the company—Indians, cowboys, and all—lined the route and heartily cheered the departing visitors.

Everything was going swimmingly, as the British say, for the 101 show in England, and Zack Miller was making plans to follow Buffalo Bill's trail throughout Europe, when storm clouds blacker than any of those that had dogged the show's trail in the spring of 1908 gathered over Europe and unleashed a fury that would change the map of the world.

One day in late summer, two policemen and four soldiers came to Zack Miller's apartment and handed him this communication:

National Emergency.
Impressment Order under Section 115
of the Army Act.

To Zack T. Miller,
68 Holland Rd. W.

His majesty, having declared that a national emergency has arisen, the horses and vehicles of the 101 Ranch Show are to be impressed for the public service, if found fit (in accordance with Section 115 of the Army Act), and will be paid for on the spot at the market value to be settled by the purchasing officer. Should you not accept the price paid as fair value, you have the right to appeal to the County Court (in Scotland the Sheriff's Court), but you must not hinder the delivery of the horses and vehicles, etc. The purchasing officer may claim to purchase such harness and stable gear as he may require with the horse or vehicle.

Charles Carpenter, Sergt.
Place Shepherd's Bush Exhibition
Date 7th August, 1914.

After the British government finished commandeering everything it wanted of the 101 show's property, all that was left were six horses, a couple of wagons, and some harnesses. For everything, Zack Miller received the equivalent of $80,000. Miller came away with more than that, however, due to the assistance of his English secretary. He considerably enhanced the value of his money by dealing in the underground currency exchange market. At the same time that the show's property had been confiscated, the British government had closed all the banks for two weeks. Many people, therefore, were desperate for British currency. The official exchange rate at the time was $4.80 American per British pound. During the bank holiday, Miller was able to exact six dollars per pound.

"... My father always said that Bill Pickett was the greatest linguist he ever knew..."

With the show out of business, Miller confronted the problem of getting his performers back home. Americans jammed steamship offices, trying to book passage, but the demand greatly exceeded the availability. Many steamship lines were afraid to make the crossing because of their fear of German submarine attacks. Miller had to send his people on several different ships, that departed on different dates over a period of weeks. He finally came back to the United States on the United States mail boat *St. Paul*. It is not known if Pickett returned on that boat or another.

Although the war prevented the 101 show from going any

farther than England, Pickett somehow managed to spend some time on the mainland. That is evidenced in the fact that the bulldogger came back from Europe speaking pretty good German. The circumstances of how he learned German are not clear. The evidence that he did learn German is contained in a letter from Will Rogers, Jr. to G.M. Carr of Tulsa, Oklahoma, in 1958. That letter states:

> I am sure glad to hear you mention Bill Pickett. I remember my father speaking of him many times. I believe it is generally recognized that he is the origi-nator of bulldogging. My father always said that Bill Pickett was the greatest linguist he ever knew. A com-pletely uneducated Negro, he seemed to have an ear for language. He went to Europe with the 101 Ranch, I believe it was—anyway he was certainly not there more than three or four months. In that time he was speaking quite adequate German. Sometime later in the United States a German count was speaking to Bill Pickett. Dad asked how Pickett's German was. The count replied, "It is the strangest thing; he speaks a very high grade of German such as you would only learn in court circles." It developed that Pickett had learned the language from the servants of the German nobility. His accent was of the very highest.

Chapter Eleven

On the Road Again

P ERHAPS IT WAS HIS ACQUAINTANCE WITH
Germans and his facility with their language that made
Bill Pickett avidly devour the news about the war. He literally couldn't get his hands on newspapers quickly
enough to keep up with the progress of the war. Maggie and he
sometimes hopped on their horses and raced the train into the
station in Bliss to get the papers. There was a prearranged sig-
nal with the train whistle that let the Picketts know when new
papers were arriving. Of course, that was not all Pickett read in
the papers. He read every word in them. Perhaps his passion
for reading had been intensified by his year of blindness, when
others had to read to him.

Pickett, as has been pointed out, had only a fifth-grade
education. But at the time that was more education than
most people from poor backgrounds had whether they were
black, white, or some other color. Often he was asked if he

were poring through the papers to see if they were saying anything about him. When he explained that he just wanted to know what was going on in the world, most of the white cowboys dismissed his response with a chuckle. After all, they didn't read much, and the Bill Pickett they thought they knew and understood was not supposed to be a thinking man. He might be the best all-around cowboy that ever was and one of the gutsiest men who ever lived, but he was still an uneducated Negro in their eyes.

The bulldogger didn't try to disabuse his colleagues of their stereotypical conceptions of him. He had sense enough to know that some of them already resented the royal treatment he and his family got around the ranch and on the show train. That resentment had manifested itself once in the form of some ground glass he discovered in a glass from which he had been drinking.

Although he worked as an ordinary ranch hand, breaking horses, taking care of the buffaloes, and whatever other work with livestock that had to be done, Pickett was in fact the star of the show. As Don Russell put it in *Wild Wild West*, referring to Zack Miller's meeting with Pickett in Fort Worth: "Zack Miller wanted the act for the editors' meeting, and Bill Pickett was the 101 Ranch star the rest of his days."

Ellsworth Collins and Alma Miller England put it even stronger in *The 101 Ranch*. They wrote: "Pickett was as much an institution with the Millers as he was with the show itself, and not just for his bulldogging ability."

Of course, when Pickett was away from the ranch or the show, he was just another Negro in a hostile racial climate to those whites who didn't know him. Once when Pickett was unloading one of his horses in a small Texas town, two locals approached him, and one asked:

"Where'd you steal that fine horse, boy?" Pickett told the man the horse was his.

The man replied: "No, you stole that horse, boy, and you better hand him over."

Pickett tried to ignore the remark and started to lead the horse away. When the man shoved him and wound up to throw a punch, Pickett delivered a powerful straight-arm blow under the man's armpit, which sent the assailant rolling on the ground groaning in pain.

When the man shoved him and wound up to throw a punch, Pickett delivered a powerful straight arm blow under the man's armpit, which sent the assailant rolling on the ground groaning in pain.

While the other man attended to his friend, Pickett calmly walked away oblivious to the stares of the stunned onlookers. When Maggie asked why he hadn't been scared of being mobbed for laying out that white man, Pickett just shrugged and said: "What's gonna happen, gonna happen."

What was not going to be anymore was the 101 show the way it had been from 1908 through the summer of 1914. The British confiscation had taken much of the show's best stock and equipment. Half of the show, however, had been left behind in the states. During winter quarters, the Millers were able to add new stock and equipment and put together a new show that opened in Hot Springs, Arkansas, in April 1915. Pickett was again in the starring role. He shared star status, however, with Jess Willard, the world's heavyweight boxing champion. On April 5 in Havana, Cuba, Willard had won the crown from Jack Johnson by virtue of a knockout in the twenty-sixth round. Although it is generally conceded today that Johnson threw that fight in exchange for being allowed to return to the United States without going to jail, most Americans of that day thought that the Great White Hope's knockout was the real thing. Crowds paid eagerly to see Willard spar with local toughs and show how he vanquished the arrogant black champion.

Pickett was showcased in both bulldogging and bronc riding during the 1915 season. That wasn't unusual. He frequently took part in other events in the show in supporting roles and to fill in for injured performers. Although Pickett's lasting reputation is based primarily on his being the inventor and most sensational practitioner of bulldogging, he was a total cowboy. He could rope and ride with the best and served as an instructor of cowboy skills at the ranch. Zack Miller described Pickett as the "greatest sweat-and-dirt cowhand that ever lived—bar none." He added, "When they turned Bill Pickett out they broke the mold."

Interestingly, Milt Hinkle who so frequently compared himself to Pickett, amended Miller's comment. Hinkle quoted Miller as having said: "When Pickett and Hinkle passed on, the mold would be broken."

The 1915 season proved profitable, and the Millers put together a 1916 show with Buffalo Bill Cody as the headliner and Pickett as the featured bulldogger. Jess Willard had moved on to the Sells-Floto Circus. The 1916 show bore the ponderous title of "Buffalo Bill (Himself) and 101 Ranch Wild West, Combined with the Military Pageant Preparedness—Presented by the Miller and Arlington Wild West Show Company."

It is noteworthy that "Brothers" did not appear in the title. The Miller brothers were at odds with each other at the time. Zack Miller, who had taken the show to England, did not tour with the 1915 and 1916 shows. The brothers also had to take turns attending to those parts of the ranch empire in which they specialized. Joe Miller being the only

Milt Hinkle who so frequently compared himself to Pickett, amended Miller's comment. Hinkle quoted Miller as having said: "When Pickett and Hinkle passed on, the mold would be broken."

brother with the show in 1916, however, did not substantially change its content. Some Arabian acrobats and gymnasts were added to match the Far East element several other shows had added. The military preparedness pageant related to the possibility that the United States was leaning toward overt involvement in World War I. That part of the show consisted of the standard United States Artillery Drill and regular members of the United States Cavalry in military exercises and horsemanship. There was also a reenactment of the Defense of Columbus, New Mexico, against

Pancho Villa's forces. On March 9, 1916, Pancho Villa lead an army of about fifteen thousand guerrillas across the U.S. border and attacked Columbus, New Mexico. Seventeen Americans were killed. U.S. soldiers chased Villa's guerrillas into Mexico, killing fifty of them on U.S. soil and seventy south of the border. Brigadier General John J. (Blackjack) Pershing, six days later, led six thousand troops into Mexico to try to find and vanquish Villa's forces.

For political reasons, the military preparedness theme had to be dropped during the show's engagement in Chicago that August. Mayor William Hale (Big Bill) Thompson did not want to risk offending the large percentage of his voters who were of German descent. Although Thompson had been a vehement proponent of military preparedness, he changed his tune after being informed that Chicago had the sixth largest German population out of all the cities of the world. To accommodate "Big Bill" and the Germans of Chicago, the "Buffalo Bill (Himself) and 101 Ranch Wild West, Combined with the Military Pageant Preparedness" became (from August 19 through August 27, 1916) the "Chicago Shan-Kive and Round-up."

This event is usually cited as the pivotal merging of the Wild West show and rodeo, and Bill Pickett appropriately competed in it. Shan-Kive supposedly translated from some Indian languages as "having a good time," and rodeo, the promoters explained, simply meant round-up in Spanish. Although the show had been a typical Wild West show before it rolled into Chicago and would revert to being one when it left the Windy City, it was a sports competition for that week, or so the promoters said.

It was, in fact, very similar to a modern-day rodeo, with rules for every event and competitions for world titles. Contestants included Hank Durnell, who had almost died of smallpox on the way to Argentina; Montana Jack Ray; Tom Kirnan; Mexican Joe; Prairie Lillie; Lucille Mulhall, the great roper and rider often cited as "the first cowgirl"; and Bill Pickett.

It was, in fact, very similar to a modern day rodeo, with rules for every event and competitions for world titles.

The rules of the bulldogging contest reflected a sensitivity to the humane societies. They said: "Positively no biting allowed." One newspaper report of the toothless bulldogging indicated that Pickett and Ed Lindsay were tied for the title with the identical time of eleven seconds on the first day of the competition. Ultimately, Pickett won the bulldogging at the Shan-Kive.

Two weeks earlier Pickett had competed at Guy Weadick's ambitious New York Stampede at Sheepshead Bay in Brooklyn and had taken twenty-two seconds to dispose of his steer. There was an altercation during the Stampede about whether or not Pickett had "hoolihaned" his steer, a practice not permitted in rodeo competitions (although Pickett sometimes did it for theatrical effect in exhibitions). In any event, Pickett did not place among the top finishers at the Stampede, which was an important event for the rodeo but a financial disaster. A polio epidemic and a subway strike combined to hold audiences far below expectations.

Two weeks after the *Shan-Kive*, Pickett won the bulldogging at the Cattleman's Carnival in Garden City, Kansas, with times of eight seconds and twelve seconds. His eight-second takedown was one second slower than the world's best for that year, which was pretty good for a forty-six-year-old man.

Chapter Twelve

Twilight on the Sawdust Trail

T THE END OF THE 1916 SEASON, THE MILLERS
folded their tents like the Bedouins and stole away from
the Wild West show business with their saddlebags stuffed
with $800,000 from the sale of the show's assets. Jess
Willard reportedly put up the bulk of the purchase money,
although the show sallied forth in 1917 under the fulsome title
"Buffalo Bill Wild West Show Co., Inc., Ray O. Archer present Jess Willard (Himself in the Flesh) and the Buffalo Bill
Wild West Show and Circus." The Miller brothers would not
allow the use of their name. It was essentially the same show as
that of the previous year, with the notable exceptions of
Buffalo Bill, whose name it carried; the Indian Iron Tail, whose
image was replicated on the buffalo nickel; and Bill Pickett.

Before the year was out the new show had passed into historical footnote-land, where most of the other Wild West
shows had already gone. Buffalo Bill died on January 10, 1917,

in Denver, and his death symbolically ended the heyday of the Wild West shows. The main factors in the demise of the quintessentially American form of show business included: the rise of new forms of transportation and entertainment; emergence of the circus behemoths; vaudeville; the movies; and rodeo.

For the remainder of his performing career, Bill Pickett was to only occasionally do any bulldogging, and most of that in rodeos. He worked at the 101 Ranch steadily until 1920, participating in rodeos there and venturing out from time to time for competitions in other places. Although he was getting on in years, the competitive urge and the zest for performing before a crowd were as strong in him as ever.

Buffalo Bill died on January 10, 1917, in Denver, and his death symbolically ended the heyday of the Wild West shows.

At the age of fifty, Pickett competed in the Dewey (Oklahoma) Roundup before a crowd of fifteen thousand and came in second in bulldogging to Milt Hinkle. Although Pickett turned in the best time on the first and third days of the roundup, his second-day steer escaped him. Hinkle won on the basis of three completed takedowns. The other competitor in that event was gored almost fatally when he lost his grip on a steer.

If Hinkle is to be believed, his victory over Pickett at the Dewey Roundup was his sixth out of six head-to-head contests against Pickett. Hinkle was always comparing himself to Pickett. He gave Pickett full credit for having invented the sport and for teaching him many of the techniques and tricks of the sport. When Hinkle became a writer he lost no opportunity to associate his name with Pickett's achievements. It was as though he sensed that Pickett's fame would endure after that of most of the other cowboy performers had been forgotten. Hinkle appears to have made a conscious effort to ensure that he would be remembered along with Pickett.

Eleven years later, Hinkle would almost die trying to eclipse Pickett in bulldogging. He tried to bulldog a steer from an airplane and wound up crippled for life.

One of the things Hinkle coveted was recognition as "the first white man ever to bulldog a steer." He greatly resented the fact that Lon Sealy had been given credit for being the first white cowboy to do it. He blamed that historical error on a 101 Ranch show press agent who played up Sealy's performance when he substituted for Pickett in the bulldogging event at the Jamestown Exhibition in 1907. Pickett was recovering from injuries at the time. Hinkle wrote:

> If he knew that same feat had been accomplished by me in Bovina, Texas, in 1904, and by Clayton Danks in Wyoming in 1906, he carefully forgot these facts to favor Sealy.

Sealy's bulldogging was, in fact, a bogus act. He didn't grapple with a big, wild, unpredictable longhorn, as was Pickett's practice. Pickett told Hinkle that Sealy dogged the same old steer at every performance and that Zack Miller came to refer to that steer as "Old Lon."

Sealy was dogging "Old Lon" when the show visited Gulfport, Mississippi, and he met his tragic end. He was doing the bulldogging because Pickett was not welcome in Gulfport. There were numerous places where Pickett was not allowed to perform because of racial prejudice. In some places masked and hooded men or police officers refused to allow the show to go on if he were in it.

Hinkle appeared to take some delight in telling about what happened to Sealy in Gulfport. He wrote:

> Sealy's career did not last long. In a case of mistaken identity in a dark railroad yard at Gulfport, Mississippi, Sealy and a deputy sheriff fired at each other simultaneously and both were killed.

That occurred during a fracas that broke out when some Gulfport Negroes were prevented from attending the show. As the disturbance grew to a near race riot, Sealy was hit with a rock. He became enraged and ran a black man down with his horse. That made matters worse. Sealy got his pistol and went out looking to shoot some of the Negroes. The deputy sheriff, who was looking to do the same thing was prowling the same area as Sealy. When the two encountered each other in the dark, they simultaneously opened fire and hit each other in the head.

Prior to his match with Hinkle at the 1920 Dewey Roundup, the fifty-year-old inventor of bulldogging had a bulldog exhibition at a rodeo in Sand Springs, Oklahoma. He mistimed his jump on his first steer and landed face-first in the sod. He was terribly scraped, cut, and bruised—so much so that his head had to be wrapped in bandages like a mummy. Nevertheless he came back out and handily disposed of his second steer.

The shower of coins with which the fans responded to that performance was more gratifying to him than any of the many others he had received during his peak years as a bull-dogger. The first time that had happened to him was in Texarkana, Arkansas, in 1904. He would always remember that day. It wasn't the money as much as it was the gratifica-tion he felt from the tribute. And he really appreciated the Sand Springs coin shower because that hadn't happened to him in a long while.

Chapter Thirteen

Empty Saddles in the Old Corral

❧

ABOUT THE TIME THAT THE MILLER BROTHERS decided to get back into the traveling show business in 1924, the fifty-five-year-old Pickett and his wife Maggie moved back to their place on the fringe of the 101 Ranch. For the previous four years they'd lived in Oklahoma City, where he had worked at the Oklahoma City Stockyards and the Southwestern Oil Mill Company. Although Pickett cherished every moment of those years in which he had more time than ever before to spend with his family, the work left him unfulfilled. He missed the traveling, the noise of the crowds, the camaraderie of the cowboys, and all the sights, sounds, and smells of life on a working ranch.

During those years, he spent hours upon hours reminiscing about the glory years, of the places he'd been, the people he'd met. The cowboy's life and show business were in his blood and always would be. He remembered old friends from the ranch and show who had gone on to make big names for themselves in moving pictures—Tom Mix, Buck Jones, and Hoot Gibson.

Pickett suspected from the day he first met Tom Mix that the former bartender and army deserter was destined for stardom. In the first place, hawk-faced, flamboyant Mix looked the part of the dime-novel cowboy people had read about.

Added to that were the fancy, dude-ranch cowboy duds he favored and his imagination and talent for selling himself. Mix made up wild stories about having been a Texas Ranger and being in shoot-outs with outlaws. He said he'd been a sheriff in Oklahoma and Kansas. He told the papers he'd been a United States Marshall from 1905 to 1910. But Pickett knew that Mix was working at the 101 Ranch in 1905 and in the 101 show during those years. Mix had known very little about the work of a cowboy when the Millers hired him from behind a bar in Oklahoma City and brought him to the ranch. But he was a fast learner and had guts.

. . . he spent hours upon hours reminiscing about the glory years, of the places he'd been, the people he'd met. The cowboy's life and show business were in his blood. . .

Years after both Pickett and Mix had gone to that great roundup in the sky, Buck Rainey in *Saddle Aces of the Cinema,* called Tom Mix:

. . . the embodiment of the world's yearning for a bigger-than-life hero—a strange, unbelievable fate for an army deserter shoving drinks across a mahogany bar

when Colonel Joe Miller blew into town for a cow-
man's convention in 1905. After a little sipping, chew-
ing and jawing, the irascible colonel hired the twenty-
two-year-old intractable kid who envisioned himself a
cowboy. For cash wages of fifteen dollars a month and
room and board, Tom went to work as a wrangler of
tenderfeet and quickly worked his way up to livestock
foreman of the vast enterprise. Before long he had won
the respect of professional cowboys, such as Bill
Pickett, and was entering rodeos and holding his own
with the best of them.

Pickett recalled when Buck Jones hooked up with the show in
Texas City, Texas, in 1913. He found out that Jones's real
name was Charles Frederick Gebhard and that he had called it
quits on a military career after the army made him an airplane
mechanic instead of a pilot.

Jones got his discharge in Texas City just at the time the
101 show happened to be playing there. Jones, who had grown
up on his father's three-thousand-acre ranch in Red Rock,
Oklahoma, hired on to curry horses. But in short order, Jones
became the show's top bronc buster. Pickett recalled that Jones
met his wife, Odelle, when the show was playing Madison
Square Garden in 1914.

Pickett was the main attraction during that New York
stand, just before the show embarked for England. *The New
York Times* referred to him as "The Famous Cowboy Bill
Pickett." It was during one of those 1914 performances, says
Colonel Bailey Hanes, that Pickett had to drag the steer out
of the grandstand.

Hoot Gibson, Pickett remembered fondly, was a genuine all-around cowboy and one of the best bulldoggers to ever follow in his boot steps. Hoot told Pickett his nickname had been slapped on him because he had a real fondness for hunting owls when he was a boy. Gibson, whose real name was Edmund Richard Gibson, was with the show as early as 1907. Bronc riding was his specialty then. But he took up bulldogging when he hitched on with the Dick Stanley-Brit Atkinson Wild West Show. Pickett was among the competitors when Gibson won the world champion cowboy belt at the Pendleton Oregon Roundup in 1912. Two years later Gibson was working for Universal Studios as a stuntman and double. In 1917, he got his first feature role.

Hoot Gibson, Pickett remembered fondly, was a genuine all-around cowboy and one of the best bulldoggers to ever follow in his bootsteps.

Pickett, too, appeared in the movies—a couple of short documentaries titled *The Bulldogger* in 1923 and *The Crimson Skull* in 1924. There is a copy of *The Bulldogger* in the Library of Congress. It shows Pickett doing his specialty as well as roping and riding, and giving instruction to other cowboys. However, he never did any acting, and he often wondered if he would have done any good in films—if that door had not been closed to him because of his race.

Still, Pickett knew that even if he had been white, his chances of making it big in motion pictures like Tom Mix, Buck Jones, or Hoot Gibson would have been slim. Those friends of his were just the lucky ones. Cowboys were a dime a dozen in the eyes of the motion picture makers. The cowboy extras were paid next to nothing and treated badly, and Pickett had no hankering for that kind of hand-to-mouth living. He did do considerable behind-the-scenes work with the motion pictures made at the ranch. He always chuckled when he remembered the time he was called upon to take the soda-water drinking bear, Tony, to the site of a shoot.

Pickett had good rapport with Tony, so getting him in the truck and carrying him to the location was supposed to be a breeze. Although the bear could be stubborn sometimes, especially when he wanted a drink and didn't get it, Pickett could usually get him to cooperate. But not that day. Tony took one look at the truck, sat down, and refused to move. Not even soda water would get him to budge. Ranch foreman Wes Rogers tried to give Pickett a hand in shoving Tony toward the truck, but there was too much bear there. His patience exhausted, Rogers decided to rope Tony and pull him into the truck. The effort was futile. Tony was too heavy for two men to move against his will. But Rogers was just as determined to load Tony into the truck as Tony was not to be loaded.

Rogers told Pickett to get into the truck and start it, which the cowboy did. Then Rogers got on his horse, tied the rope to the saddle horn, rode around to the front of the truck, and urged his horse forward. Even Tony could not resist that pressure. He got up, lost his balance, and flew forward with such momentum that he continued right through the back of the open-cockpit truck and into the front seat beside Pickett. It was a tight fit, and

Pickett was almost pushed out of the truck. But he decided to leave well enough alone. He patted the gas and took off. There they went down the road, two bosom buddies, side by side, a little brown man and a big brown bear out for a morning spin.

Pickett also enjoyed the Sunday rodeos at the ranch. These were not piddling affairs. All the contestants were first-rate riders, ropers, and bulldoggers, and the Millers went to great lengths to make the rodeos as enjoyable and exciting as major competitions. It was during one of those 101 rodeos that the great lady trick-and-bronc rider Florence Reynolds got her start in that dangerous avocation. She told of her association with Pickett in the book *The Rawhide Tree*. Here is her account of her first ride at the 101 on a wild one named Kelly:

> I climbed the chute fence and straddled over the little bay named Kelly. From the instructions I received from the hands, I could tell they knew I was green. . . My knees were weak and I was trembling, but I just had to ride that horse! . . . When the chute gate opened and Kelly started out my stage fright was gone. But I was entertained plenty. Kelly sun-fished first on one side and then on the other.
>
> Bill Pickett was my pick-up man, and he was a good one! When he lifted me off, he said, "Ma'am, you're good! That horse shore did buck!" Everybody on the ranch liked Bill. He didn't talk much, and the words of praise he had for me made me feel fine! The others smiled and waved approval. "You were great!" they said.

Reynolds also needed Pickett's help when she tried to ride a wild horse named Possum. The horse had almost torn up the chute trying to get out. Possum created such a stir that Zack Miller told Pickett to take him out into the arena and "snub him." Pickett rode Possum enough to take some of the thunder out of the temperamental horse. Then he brought him back and managed to control the horse long enough for Reynolds to mount him by clamping his teeth onto the horse's ear.

Such reminiscences aside, it felt good to Pickett to be back at the ranch doing the kind of work he liked and helping to prepare the stock for the new show. The Millers had actually considered hitting the sawdust trail again a year earlier, but a one-hundred-year flood hit the ranch in late June of that year, causing a temporary setback.

The new show was the biggest and most extravagant the Millers had ever put on the road. Thirty steel railroad cars were required to transport everything. Miller Brothers had a private car that some described as "a palace on wheels." It even had a library. The bandwagon was framed with huge wood engravings depicting works known as *Aztec Sacrifice* and *The Landing of Ponce de Leon*. Some of the best rodeo talent in the nation was assembled for it, including Milt Hinkle. In addition, the Millers hired:

— a troupe of Cossack riders from Russia
— dancing girls from the Ziegfield Follies, Mexico City, Havana, Buenos Aires, New Orleans, and the Far East
— a team of Arab acrobats
— animal acts that, in addition to Brahma bulls and wild horses, included elk, camels, and elephants

Although Pickett did not travel with the show, he was in the parade when the roving extravaganza hit Oklahoma City on April 21, 1925. That parade consisted of forty wagon loads of people and livestock. The Millers spared no expense to make the show a success, but it was doomed to failure. It played to good audiences in 1925 and brought in substantial gross revenue, but expenses sopped up the profits. The show had barely broken even when it limped home at the end of that year, and worse was to come.

The new show was the biggest and most extravagant the Millers had ever put on the road. Thirty steel railroad cars were required to transport everything. Miller Brothers had a private car that some described as "a palace on wheels." It even had a library.

In addition to the costs of paying, feeding, and transporting five hundred performers, they faced fierce competition from other traveling shows, principally the Ringling Brothers Circus and the Sell-Floto Circus. That competition often approached the level of all-out war. Advance agents from those shows tore down 101 broadsheets and sent goon squads to provoke fights with 101 canvas riggers and to start panics during the shows.

The Millers also resorted to dirty tricks. One of those battles was in Virginia when they spread the rumor that much of the Ringling Brothers livestock had picked up hoof-and-mouth disease during a Texas tour. Forty thousand Virginians signed a petition urging that Ringling Brothers be prohibited from playing in Virginia. The governor of Virginia banned the circus from the state. Uncontested in

Virginia, the 101 show cleaned up. Although they won the battle, they lost the war. The show ended the season more than $100,000 in the red.

Joe Miller was still determined to make the show a success, but the effort took its toll on him physically and emotionally. He lapsed periodically into black moods, and both the hair on his head and his thick brush mustache turned white. He poured more and more of his money into the show. The other brothers followed suit and also invested heavily. The show failed to make money again in 1927.

On the afternoon of October 21, 1927, Colonel Joe Miller was found dead of carbon monoxide poisoning in the garage of his home. Reports indicated that it was an accidental death. He had last been seen at the ranch at about 10:00 A.M., when he put some groceries in his car to take to his home about five miles away. He had picked up the groceries because his wife was due to return with their infant son from a visit to her old home in Grand Rapids, Michigan.

Miller's car reportedly was giving him some trouble when he left the ranch. He appeared to have been working on it. The garage doors were partly open, the hood of the car was up, and his pocketknife was on the running board. One theory is that he started the motor to try to ascertain the problem and was overcome by the fumes.

Bill Pickett was among the more than five thousand show people, cowboys, ranchers, Indians, politicians, and business leaders who attended Colonel Joe Miller's funeral on the front porch of the White House. Joe Miller had been a dear friend and benefactor to Pickett for more than twenty-two years, and his death cut him like a knife.

Joe Miller had been the driving force behind the new show, and his death appeared to be the grand finale for the Millers in show business. Zack and George Miller tried to keep the show going for a while, pouring more and more of their assets into the money pit and neglecting the ranch in the process. George made increasingly risky investments in the oil business in hopes of making a killing that would keep the diversified empire afloat.

Zack Miller thought the most prudent thing to do was to unload the show. He almost had that done, but George balked at the sale when the prospective buyer insisted on the right to use the Miller name in promoting the show. Zack had no choice but to take the show on the road again, and things continued to go from bad to worse. In addition to mounting operating expenses and the competition, the show was hit with an epidemic of lawsuits lodged by people who claimed injuries or damages caused by the show.

Then, when it appeared things couldn't get any worse, tragedy struck again on February 1, 1929. Colonel George Miller's car skidded on a patch of ice as he was coming home from Ponca City. The accident occurred about 2:00 A.M., and it was 4:00 A.M. before the wreckage was discovered. George Miller died before he reached the hospital. Once again, Pickett grieved over an empty saddle in the 101 corral. He had not been as close to George Miller as he had been to Colonel Joe, but he liked and respected the low-key, all-business middle Miller brother.

One month later, Bill Pickett would be in his deepest mourning about another empty saddle—a deeper grief than he could ever have imagined cut into the core of his being. Maggie Pickett, the only woman he had ever loved or ever would, died on March 14, 1929. All their daughers had married and moved away. He was left alone in the big house on his 160-acre spread near Chandler with the memories of his family and the painful regret that his career had kept him from spending more time with them. Wherever he had traveled, in his mind was the image of Maggie the way she was when they first met. That is how he envisioned her now. Something inside him assured him that her spirit would always be with him, although her body was at rest a few miles away in Norman.

Chapter Fourteen

....

The Last Roundup

I F BILL PICKETT HAD BEEN A CRYING MAN,
he would have released a flood of hot tears when the
remains of the great 101 Ranch Wild West Show were
returned to the ranch in 1931. What was left of what had
been one of the greatest traveling entertainment units ever
assembled was now, at best, poor salvage. A couple of elephants and a few steers and horses were all that remained of
the livestock. The show wagons looked as though they had
been picked up and dropped by a tornado. The once-magnifi-
cent bandwagon capsulized the calamity. It had been ravaged
so badly that the *The Landing of Ponce de Leon* and *Aztec
Sacrifice* engravings were unrecognizable. The images had literally been gouged and scraped out. The big tent had been torn
to ribbons, as were the gorgeous harnesses and saddles. The
huge ornate mirrors were shattered. Every vehicle was disman-
tled and the luxurious cars were in shambles.

The demise of the show hit Pickett like a sledgehammer, although he had not traveled with it for years. He was sixty-one years old and his bulldogging days were over. Still, he was with the show in spirit as he went about his chores at the ranch. When he heard about the performers running amok and tearing up the equipment in Washington, D. C., he was stunned. Still, he could understand their feelings, if they couldn't get their pay.

It was that depression Pickett kept reading about in the newspapers. He didn't completely understand the phenomenon, but he did know that people were out of work all over the place and rich men were jumping out of the windows of tall office buildings. He also knew that Zack Miller was way over his head in debt and about to come apart at the seams from trying to hold things together. He knew that the ranch had plenty of livestock and a good harvest of crops. The problem was that no one had any money, and the ranch couldn't sell any of their livestock or produce.

The same thing, Pickett figured, had gone wrong with the show. People just didn't have the money to buy tickets. He had heard the colonel voice suspicions that the show was being sabotaged by the man he'd taken on to run it, a man named Charles Bulware. This Bulware continually pressed Miller for more and more money to keep the show going, but the show kept losing money as fast as Miller could pump it into it. Colonel Miller came to the conclusion that Bulware had made a deal with the big circus conglomerates to bleed the 101 show to death by booking it in the wrong places at the wrong times, scheduling stops long distances away from each other to drive up freight costs, and by providing inade-quate advanced publicity.

When the show arrived in Washington, D. C., in 1931, no one knew it was coming, and it got there three months later than the best time for business in that city. That confirmed Miller's suspicions that someone had paid Bulware to ruin the show. Of course, he couldn't prove that. Nevertheless, when Bulware wired for money, Miller refused and ordered him to pack up everything and bring the show home.

Told that no money was coming, the performers, who hadn't been paid in a month, became enraged and smashed everything they could get to with axes, sledgehammers, crowbars, and sticks. The show was no more, and as far as Pickett could see, it would not rise again from those ruins.

Told that no money was coming, the performers, who hadn't been paid in a month, became enraged and smashed everything they could get to with axes, sledgehammers, crowbars, and sticks. The show was no more . . .it would not rise again from those ruins.

With the show gone, Pickett worried about the future of the ranch. It was not his, of course, but it was home. After Maggie died, Pickett moved out of their large house near Chandler into a small house on the ranch near the headquarters.

Creditors were clawing at Zack Miller like hungry vultures. Things went downhill in a hurry when, in the fall of 1931, Joe Miller's son George W. Miller and the Exchange Trust

Company of Tulsa, which represented George's heirs, succeeded in getting the managing of the ranch turned over to a receiver. Pickett didn't understand the legal niceties of receivership but he could see the effects. The receiver, Fred C. Clarke, a rancher near Winfield, leased out 101 grassland and farm property. He fired most of the old cowhands and hired cheap, inexperienced laborers. He sold most of the equipment and farm tools and machinery. He cut a deal with his son-in-law for the 101's corn crop. He allowed livestock to graze in the orchard Luther Burbank had donated to Joe Miller, and the animals had destroyed it.

With the receivership, Miller's problems became insurmountable. His litigants and creditors swarmed all over him, and he could not use any income from the ranch to try to hold them at bay. He cracked under the pressure and had to be confined to bed under a doctor's care.

Then came the black day when the 101 went on the auction block. Clarke had advertised the auction for March 24, 1932, and Pickett was sent with a couple of other hands to separate the horses that were to be sold from the few Miller would be allowed to keep. Pickett approached his task with a heavy heart, because he knew how what was happening had to be tearing at Zack Miller's guts.

He really feared that Miller would lose his mind. In the last conversation he had with the colonel, Miller had raved about the two of them going to Africa and starting over in the cattle business. Well, Pickett knew he was too old to even dream of doing anything like that. And he never wanted to be somewhere too far away that he couldn't be brought back and buried within waving distance of where Maggie was resting. She was buried in Norman after her fatal brain hemorrhage.

As they approached the corral, Pickett picked out a half-wild four-year-old sorrel that was acting up and looking like a real challenge. That horse looked so familiar to Pickett. He reminded him of a horse he'd had the devil trying to gentle when he and his brothers were in the bronc-busting business down in Taylor, Texas. The animal went into a frenzy when Pickett looped his rope around its neck. It reared pawing the air, grazed Pickett's head, and knocked him from his horse, but Pickett still felt he had the situation under control. Even at sixty-two he still believed himself to be more than a match for any creature with four hooves. He began walking toward the horse, tightening the rope hand-over-hand, clicking his teeth, and murmuring ever so softly, "Come to old Bill, boy. Come to old Bill." Suddenly the horse made an unpredictable lunge and pulled Pickett off his feet. Then the animal kicked him solidly in the head, producing a crunching sound.

They drove Pickett to a hospital in Ponca City as fast as they could, but he never regained consciousness. He lay in a

The animal went into a frenzy when Pickett looped his rope around its neck. It reared pawing the air, grazed Pickett's head and knocked him from his horse . . .

coma emitting muffled sounds from time to time and flinching every now and then as though he were struggling. Perhaps he was remembering the more than six thousand steers he had dogged during his days or Frijoli Chiquita.

While Bill Pickett lay in a coma, Zack Miller was going through hell. The *Daily Oklahoman* reported the proceeding of that fateful day of the auction, March 24, 1932:

> There were sad doings here Thursday, marking the pas-
> sage of a great Oklahoma institution, the 101 Ranch,
> internationally famous symbol of a young state that
> rides 'em cowboy. A picturesque crowd of more than
> three thousand persons turned out for the receiver's sale
> of the property of the Miller brothers' 101 Ranch Trust,
> a few coming to buy, but a vast majority simply to walk
> stolidly along the dusty lanes and watch with calm
> solicitude the disintegration of the greatest show place
> in the West.
>
> Over in the historic White House of the ranch,
> Colonel Zack Miller, sole survivor of the trio of broth-
> ers which made the place famous, roared defiance at
> the world, threatening to blow up the mansion, and
> even fired a shotgun in the direction of attorneys seek-
> ing a conference with him. He termed the sale a "legal
> robbery."

The article went on to describe the auctioning of the live-stock, farm machinery, and other properties and the emotional reaction of the spectators. It adds:

> "The lonely old man there in the famous White House,
> living among his dead hopes, bellowing defiance from

his sickbed, simply typified the already half-forgotten glamorous yesterdays of Oklahoma."

Eight days later, on April 2, 1932, Bill Pickett let go of the horns of this mortal state of being. They held his funeral on the steps of the White House, where Joe Miller also had been so honored and the crowds had gathered a few days earlier to witness the death throes of the Miller brothers' empire. Hundreds attended the rites, a rainbow mixture of blacks, whites, Indians, cowboys, farmers, ranch hands, friends, and family.

After the Reverend S. Sylvester Fairley of St. John's Baptist Church in Ponca City eulogized Pickett, the choir called for a "sweet chariot" to "swing low" and carry his spirit home. Then they buried his body on a windy knoll in a good coffin inside a hardwood box in hard ground so the coyotes couldn't scratch up his bones. And Will Rogers told the world on the radio and in *The New York Times* that the inventor of bulldogging was gone.

Bill Pickett was buried on a wind-whipped knoll about a half-mile to the north of the southern boundary of the 101 Ranch, i.e., on land that once was part of the great ranch empire. More precisely, the grave is about a quarter of a mile east of U.S. Highway 77 and about three miles south of the old ranch headquarters. Pickett is in good company there. The great Ponca chief White Eagle, whose gesture of gratitude allowed the Millers to build their multifaceted economic domain, is buried no more than fifty feet away.

Only five years before his fatal accident, Pickett had attended a special memorial service at White Eagle's grave. White Eagle died in 1914. In 1927, the Millers erected a fourteen-foot-high red sandstone monument to him. The monument said:

Indian Trail Marker
Re-erected to the memory of
CHIEF WHITE EAGLE
(1840-1914)
Who led his people to civilization
And favored the White Man's ways
Erected by Miller Brothers
101 Ranch, June 1927.

Pickett, although well into his fifties, had the stamina and agility of a man in his thirties. He could hardly have imagined that less than five years later, he would be interred so soon so close to White Eagle. But then Pickett had told a reporter in Phoenix, Arizona, in 1904 that someday he might make a fatal mistake.

It would be four years before a suitable marker would be placed on Bill Pickett's grave. What was finally put there was just what Pickett would have wanted, a simple upright sandstone slab with the inscription "Bill Pickett, C.S.C.P.A." The Cherokee Strip Cowpunchers Association, of which Pickett was the only black member, erected it.

Although he had been near death at the time of Pickett's death, Zack Miller survived for twenty more years. When Pickett was kicked in the head by the horse, Miller flew into a rage, blaming those controlling the affairs of the ranch for Pickett's death, asserting that it would not have happened if they had kept experienced hands to help him separate the horses. He continued in that vein until the funeral, which he attended against his doctor's orders. After the funeral, he grew gravely ill, and ten days later, the doctors' prognosticated that he would not survive to see another dawn.

Then came the Ponca medicine men of the peyote-eating sect, led by chief medicine man Jim Williams. They forced their way into Miller's sickroom and ordered the removal of all white man's medicine, syringes, and medical equipment.

Squatting in the center of the room, Jim Williams poured out a bag of sand and molded it into the shape of a heart. He started a small fire in front of the sand on a grass mat, on which the Indians already had arranged eagle feathers and cedar branches. Smoke ascended in serpentine swirls, and Jim Williams rose slowly with it, his arms outstretched. Meanwhile, staccato beats of rawhide drums downstairs filled the house with such hypnotic sounds that Zack Miller felt that either the drums were inside his head or his head was inside one of the drums.

Then came the Ponca medicine men of the peyote-eating sect, led by chief medicine man Jim Williams. They forced their way into Miller's sickroom and ordered the removal of all white man's medicine, syringes, and medical equipment.

Finally Jim Williams said in the Ponca language: "Zack Miller, you are a sick man, and the white man's medicine cannot save you. You are our friend; so now we bringing you the faith cure."

The Indians began chanting in a way that vaguely reminded Miller of old Sits-on-a-Hill's rain-stopping incantation at the National Editorial Convention show twenty-seven years earlier. As the chanting and the drumbeats resounded, Jim Williams forced him to swallow a cup of peyote brew. It was bitter as gall. It was a struggle, but he held it down. Then the medicine man made him drink another cup, and another and another. He gave him a button of peyote to chew that was even more bitter than the drink.

Zack Miller felt like his head was going to burst open as Jim Williams called his attention to the ashes in the fire that were transforming themselves into a small pink flower. A bird zipped in through the window and perched on the flower. Jim Williams threw his head back and chanted to the beat of the drums. He reached across Miller and raised his hands ever so slowly, and Miller felt himself rise off the bed and hang suspended there. Jim Williams slowly lowered his hands and brought Miller back to rest on the bed. He then told Miller that an old friend had come to see him.

The apparition of an old friend named Jimmy Moore, who had been dead for at least forty years, came and began filling his pipe with tobacco. Moore reached into the fire, extracted a coal, sucked on his pipe, and exhaled a column of smoke that filled the room, obscuring everything and everybody.

Miller awoke twelve hours later, starving and bellowing for food.

At the Texas Centennial Celebration in Pampa, Texas in 1936, Florence Reynolds spotted Zack Miller riding in the street parade and showing off Joe Miller's $8,000 saddle. Reynolds was overjoyed to see Miller, who appeared not to recognize her at first. When he came to the realization of who she was, Miller said: "Well what do you know, our old bronc-rider, Mrs. Reynolds." When she began to press him about the 101, he stopped her.

"Don't ask me, Mrs. Reynolds! The 101 is gone. . ."

"Don't ask me, Mrs. Reynolds! The 101 is gone . . . Went broke! You remember our old friend Bill Pickett?"

When she replied in the affirmative, Miller said:

"He's dead . . . They couldn't take my horses under Oklahoma law. I was sick in bed and Bill was out there trying to separate out my horses. One of them pawed him in the head!. . .We buried him on the 101 not far from the grave of Chief White Eagle."

Chapter Fifteen

Posthumous Honors Abound

WHEN THE UNITED STATES POSTAL SERVICE decided which persons to honor posthumously in its "Legends of the West" issue, the series would not have lived up to its name had it not included a portrait of Bill Pickett. Few persons from out of that past of thundering hoofbeats, clouds of dust, and bawling cattle can lay better claim to their status as a legendary figure.

Historical correctness, of course, required some symbolic representation of African Americans in the series, but that is not the overriding reason for Pickett's inclusion. Pickett was black with a strain of Native American in his background. As such, he must be viewed as an exemplar of the contributions of black cowboys to the economy and culture of the West. Between a fourth and a fifth of the forty thousand cowboys who trailed herds of cattle up from Texas and New Mexico to the railheads in Kansas were black. In a typical trail crew of eight cowboys, two of them usually would be black. Often they were the cook and the wrangler, but most black cowboys could do it all. The majority of them had previously been slaves, whose duties included tending cattle, branding, and roping. Some had been freed by the emancipation, escaped slavery, or were born free men.

Compared to most other pursuits open to them at the time, the life of a black cowboy was not bad. Wages of cowboys were equal, regardless of race; although few black cowboys were promoted to trail boss or foreman. Living accommodations on the trail and in the bunkhouses on the ranches were roughly equal as well. Most of the saloons in the cow towns served both black and white cowboys; although in some cases at different ends of the bar.

Few of the black cowboys are remembered by name. The braggart Nat Love, also known as Deadwood Dick, and the cattle rustler Isom Dart are notable exceptions because of their infamous reputations. One of the good guys whose name has almost achieved household familiarity was Bose Ikard who worked for Charles Goodnight, founder of the Goodnight-Loving Trail. Goodnight trusted Ikard so much that he entrusted all the money to him when he couldn't get it to a bank. Black cowboys also participated in rodeos, mainly their own separate rodeos, because white cowboys preferred not to compete with them. Of those who competed in the bigger rodeos, none achieved Pickett's status. Bronc buster Jessie Stahl, however, was once generally considered the best in the world at riding wild horses.

There is ample justification, therefore, for including a Pickett portrait in the stamp series to symbolize the role of the uncelebrated black cowboy who for so much of the century was largely unacknowledged by both the history books and the mass entertainment media. That, however, is not the overriding reason for his selection. Pickett belongs in the "Legends" because he was one of the greatest of all the cowboys. Indeed, many insist that he was without debate the greatest all-around work and show business cowboy ever to straddle a horse. Pickett would have deserved his own stamp if he had been white or Hispanic. He was the quintessence of the American cowboy. Had he not been black, he would have been inducted posthumously in the National Rodeo Cowboy Hall of Fame long before 1971—thirty-nine years after his death.

Had he not been black, he would have been inducted posthumously in the National Rodeo Cowboy Hall of Fame long before 1971— thirty-nine years after his death.

It was in recognition of Pickett's extraordinary achievements as a cowboy and showman that the North Fort Worth Historical Society commissioned a bronze statue to honor him. That statue, which was unveiled in 1987, graces the front lawn of the restored Cowtown Coliseum, where Pickett was a hit with the 101's show in 1916. Zack Miller hailed the crowds that jammed all of the performances during the Fort Worth Stock Show as the biggest he'd ever seen for a city of Fort Worth's size. Pickett also did his famous act during the grand opening of the historic building in 1908— and he participated in the first indoor rodeo there in 1918.

The statue, created by Azle, Texas, artist Lisa Perry, is a 1,400-pound, nine-by-ten-foot representation of Pickett throwing a one-thousand-pound longhorn. That was about the average size of the animals Pickett and bulldoggers of his era manhandled. Today's steer wrestling events feature animals that weigh between four and five hundred pounds.

The association paid for the statue by selling a limited edition of one hundred small bronze replicas of the original at $1,750 each. Association president Sue McCafferty said at the time: "We felt like there should be something commemorating the cowboy that's all-inclusive." Bill Pickett, she said, was chosen to represent the American cowboy (not just the black cowboy) because "He went the full circle, and we feel that his life tells the story of the cowboy . . . Bill Pickett grew up doing ranch work, did his bulldogging exhibitions at Wild West shows, rode in professional rodeos, and died on the 101 Ranch."

Perry, the sculptress, commented: "All of the other rodeo events cannot be attributed to one person, but Bill Pickett is solely responsible for inventing bulldogging."

At the time of this printing a group of Fort Worth business and civic leaders were laying plans for a "Bill Pickett Suite" in the historic Stockyards Hotel in Fort Worth's Stockyards tourist area. The hotel is located about twenty yards from the statue.

As has been mentioned previously, Bill Pickett is the only black cowboy who has been inducted into the National Rodeo Cowboy Hall of Fame in Oklahoma City. He also has been inducted in the Pro Rodeo Hall of Fame in Colorado Springs, Colorado. There is a memorial to him across from the city hall in Taylor, Texas. That city held a special celebration honoring Pickett's life in 1992. A Bill Pickett display also is included in the Black in Wax Museum in Baltimore, Maryland.

A black rodeo competition bearing Pickett's name makes an annual circuit of eight to eleven cities around the nation and serves as a kind for springboard for black cowboys who are striving to advance into the bigger competitions sponsored by the Professional Rodeo Cowboys Association. Currently, there are less than one hundred card-carrying black P.R.C.A. cowboys.

All of those honors notwithstanding, the twenty-nine-cent Bill Pickett stamp is the crowning posthumous honor for the daring cowboy.

All of those honors notwithstanding, the twenty-nine-cent Bill Pickett stamp is the crowning posthumous honor for the daring cowboy. He is being honored in some very select company. Other historical figures in the pane are:

— Buffalo Bill (William Frederick Cody), the famous scout, showman, and dime-novel hero who came to personify the American Wild West to people all over the world. Buffalo Bill's shows toured Europe for several years, during which he met and performed for many of the royal families. During his last of several farewell tours of the United States, Buffalo Bill was part of the 101 Ranch show with Pickett.

— Jim Bridger, the great mountain man, guide, scout, and trapper was the first white man to set eyes on the Great Salt Lake.

— Annie Oakley (Phoebe Anne Moses), the famous female rifle shot who dazzled crowds with the Buffalo Bill Wild West Show and was the heroine of the Broadway musical "Annie Get Your Gun." Pickett and she also were occasionally on the same program.

— Chief Joseph, the great Nez Percé leader who resisted efforts by settlers to drive his people from their extensive grazing lands in Montana and resettle them on a reservation in Idaho. General Oliver Otis Howard regarded Chief Joseph as a great soldier and diplomat. Stories about Chief Joseph caused settlers to refer to him as a "red Napoleon."

— Bat Masterson, the celebrated lawman, gambler, buffalo hunter, and newspaperman, who has been the subject of numerous books and movies of varying quality. He was a friend of Buffalo Bill, Wyatt Earp, Doc Holliday, and Luke Short. Holliday was working with Luke Short in the White Elephant Saloon in Fort Worth, Texas, when Short killed Jim Courtright in a gunfight.

— John C. Frémont, the great soldier and explorer, whose explorations changed the picture of the American West. Fremont was a leader in the successful Bear Flag Rebellion of the Americans in California against Mexico. Frémont ran for president and was defeated by James Buchanan. He lost out to Abraham Lincoln in a bid for the Republican Party's presidential nomination.

— Wyatt Earp of Dodge City, Tombstone, and O. K. Corral fame. According to some accounts Earp was an exemplary lawman and champion of right and justice; other accounts protrayed him as an opportunistic, self-promoting scoundrel and killer.

— Nellie Cashman, a dynamic Irish immigrant

woman, philanthropist, and entrepreneur who made her mark as a restaurateur and gold prospector in Arizona and the Klondike.

— Charles Goodnight, scout, Texas Ranger, and rancher who blazed the Goodnight-Loving Trail from Alamagordo Creek, New Mexico, to Granada, Colorado. After moving his cattle holdings to the Texas Panhandle, Goodnight partnered with John G. Adair to found what was to become the J. A. Ranch, a one million-acre spread that ran one hundred thousand head of cattle. Goodnight developed the first blooded herds by introducing Hereford bulls.

— Geronimo, the Apache Chief who has been vilified and glorified in scores of movies. The great Apache war hero shot his last buffalo from an automobile during the National Editorial Association Convention show at the 101 Ranch in 1905. Pickett was in that show.

— Kit Carson, mountain man, scout, soldier, and Indian agent who guided Frémont on three expeditions through the Rockies, the Great Basin, and California.

— Wild Bill Hickok, gunfighter, stagecoach driver, lawman, and dime-novel hero who was assassinated in Deadwood, Dakota Territory while holding a poker hand of aces and eights. Hickok's gunfighter image derived from a gun duel in Wild Rock Creek Stage Station, Nebraska, where he single-handedly killed three men and a similar incident on the main street of Springfield, Missouri.

— Jim Beckworth, the black mountain man, scout, trapper, fur trader, rancher, hotel owner, prospector, and adventurer who found the Beckworth Pass through the Sierras to the California gold fields. Beckworth, the son of Irish aristocrat Sir Jennings Beckworth and his slave mistress, lived for six years with the Crow Indians and married several Blackfoot, Snake, and Crow women.

— Bill Tilgham, the Oklahoma lawman who got off to a bad start on the wrong side of the law with a gang of horse thieves in Kansas before settling down to earn a reputation as an exemplary lawman in Dodge City. He moved on to Oklahoma when the Cherokee Strip was opened in 1893. As sheriff of Lincoln County in 1900, he was sent on a mission to Mexico by President Theodore Roosevelt to apprehend a fugitive. In 1898, when two innocent Indian youths were lynched by a mob for an alleged rape and murder of a white woman, Tilgham arrested the members of the mob and secured convictions and prison sentences on eight of them.

— Sacagawea, the Shoshoni Indian woman who served as interpreter, guide, and diplomat for the Lewis and Clark expedition.

. . . the United States Postal Service has truly and definitively brought the extraordinary cowboy out of the shadows of history.

In associating Bill Pickett with such legendary figures, the United States Postal Service has truly and definitively brought the extraordinary cowboy out of the shadows of history. Pickett descendants, western lore enthusiasts, and stamp collectors would have been overjoyed, except for one little thing . . .

Chapter Sixteen

The Wrong Bill Pickett

T HE UNITED STATES POSTAL SERVICE SET OUT to honor a rare human being, not to create a philatelic rarity, when it decided to depict Bill Pickett in its "Legends of the West" issue. It did both, and in doing the latter it stirred up the biggest storm to shake up the world of stamp collectors in decades.

That twenty-nine-cent Bill Pickett stamp was a marvelous piece of portraiture, something every admirer of the legendary cowboy and every descendant of the Pickett clan should have been proud to collect and stick on a letter. There was just one little problem with the stamp. The picture on it was not Bill Pickett. Not only did the stamp not look like him, indeed, it bore a striking resemblance to Bill's brother Ben Pickett. In fact it was Ben, and Ben didn't look like Bill at all. The mistake shook up the sedate world of stamp collecting worse than the contention over the design of the Elvis Presley stamp.

Those "Legends" panes, which included the portrait of Ben Pickett, were supposed to go on sale in March 1994. Three months earlier some of them were released to three hundred post offices around the nation. Those early releases were standard practice for the United States Postal Service. Nearly two hundred panes, sheets of twenty stamps, including all of the honorees and four western landscape scenes were actually sold before the mistake was detected. Most of the 104,020,000 individual stamps, divided into 5,201,000 panes were sent to the 137 stamp distribution offices, the Kansas City, Missouri, fulfillment office, and about three hundred big city post offices and were not distributed before the problem came to light.

Frank S. Phillips Jr., great-grandson of Bill Pickett, a resident of Silver Springs, Maryland, and a systems analyst with the Thurgood Marshall Justice Center, informed the United States Postal Service of the misrepresentation. Phillips had learned of the mix-up when he was called about it by an Oklahoma City public television station, which was following up on a news story about the stamp snafu in the *Daily Oklahoman*. Phillips told Postmaster General Marvin T. Runyon in no uncertain terms that the portrait on the stamp was not Bill Pickett and that the distribution of the "Legends" issue should be stopped for the sake of historical accuracy.

"Living people knew Bill Pickett and can verify the picture on the stamp is wrong—like my father and some of the cousins," said Phillips. "Dad is seventy-eight, so he was nineteen when

Bill Pickett died in 1932. He taught my dad how to rope and bulldog, and all those things," he said.

In all, 250 million of the stamps had been printed, and Runyon had them all recalled on January 18. The value of the estimated 183 panes that got away immediately skyrocketed, triggering turmoil in the stamp collecting world and eliciting vehement cries for Runyon's head to roll. Wild rumors flew of each pane's value soaring to $100,000, and collectors expressed deep concern that they would not be able to complete their American collections because of the rarity that had been created. Almost every issue of the weekly newspaper *Linn's Stamp News* for the next six months carried some commentary or report about the "Legends" issue.

January 24: Lead story tells of "Legends" stamps being used as early as December 14 out of the Bend, Oregon, post office; how the artist made the mistake from a mislabeled photograph; of a man named Jim Piske of Oregon receiving a parcel while he was in Georgia with a "Legends" pane affixed to it. That edition also contained Runyon's recall statement. It read in part: "Bill Pickett was a leader in western culture whose efforts brought cowboy art to millions of Americans . . . We have a strong system to select stamp subjects. Unfortunately in this case, we found the design, research, and validation process was not followed thoroughly."

February 7: Four front-page stories and four more inside stories along with commentaries. The lead story is on the details of the recall. Another speculates on how much the rare, erroneous panes could be worth. Another suggests that there is something wrong with the Wyatt Earp stamp, as well. A commentary on page three calls for reselling the error-marred panes through the mail order philatelic service in Kansas City. It goes on to make this point:

"It's ironic that Bill Pickett is a black man, because black Americans on stamps is (sic) currently one of the fastest growing United States collecting specialties. United States Postal Service's destruction of the Pickett stamp, if successful, will make completeness in this area impossible."

February 17: An article about a Princeton student who sold a "Legends" pane for two thousand dollars. That issue also contains letters from readers suggesting that Runyon fire the clerk who sold the stamps in Bend, Oregon; advising against the recall, and suggesting that U.S.P.S. tighten up on its policy of early releases. Another commentary urged the postal service to ship new releases to post offices in wrappers that clearly indicate when they are to be put on sale.

February 21: A whole page of letters advised against the recall and suggested that all of the panes be released to prevent the creation of an expensive rarity.

February 28: An ad appeared stating, "Gary Posner Has It!! The Only Known Mint 'Bill Pickett Sheet'!!! Buying or selling, Gary Posner, Inc. is your best source."

March 7: Lead story tells of a United States education adviser in Brazil who bought a dozen "Legends" panes in Princeton, New Jersey, in January and used the stamps on mail dispatched from Brazil. Other stories tell of upcoming new "Legends" designs; a "Legends" pane to be auctioned in April; and finding no serious problem with the Annie Oakley stamp.

April 4: Front-page story on U.S. Representative William L. Clay, a Democrat from Missouri, on his efforts to get all the erroneous "Legends" panes released. Issuing the recalled stamps, Clay said, would "eliminate the incentive for printing erroneous stamps."

April 25: Stories on discoveries of canceled Nellie Cashman, Sacagawea, and a Native American culture stamps.

May 2: A wrap-up story on "Legends" pointing out that a mint pane found in McLean, Virginia, was sold at auction for $4,620 and that a pane bought from a Princeton student for $5,000 was sold to dealer Gary Posner on the same day for $12,500.

And the beat went on.

In June, the postal service decided on a compromise to try to calm the furor. The service announced that it would issue one hundred fifty thousand of the Ben Pickett stamps and distribute a whole new issue of "Legends" with the correct Bill Pickett portrait. That compromise was reached through negotiations between Azeezaly S. Jaffer, manager of the postal service stamp service, and Phillips, who had been adamant about not wanting the erroneous stamp to go down through history as representing his great-grandfather. Phillips had said in other contexts that his seventy-eight-year-old father, a retired rodeo cowboy, was furious about the mistake.

Jaffer convinced Phillips that not releasing any more of the stamps would make the few that had been sold so valuable that their rarity would assume more historical significance than the honor being bestowed upon Bill Pickett.

On June 6, Phillips sent a letter agreeing to a compromise to Postmaster General Runyon. That letter is reprinted here.

Dear Mr. Runyon:

Once again, thank you for setting the record straight on Bill Pickett. I recently met with members of your staff who inform me that in the past few months the Postal Service has come under great pressure to release the recalled Legends of the West stamps. The unfortunate sale of the stamps has created a rarity in the stamp collecting world and collectors are insisting that the Legends sheets bearing the incorrect image be sold in order to complete their collections.

While I have previously written to you expressing my feelings on this issue, Mssrs. Jaffer and Tolbert discussed the possibility of releasing a limited number of stamps through mail order from your fulfillment operation in Kansas City. I understand that these stamps would be displayed in a protective sleeve with a clear message to collectors that they are to be saved and not intended for use. Given the choice, I would prefer that the stamps not be sold, but in light of compromising the world-wide hobby of stamp collecting and unnecessarily inflating the value of the incorrect sheets in the marketplace today, the Postal Service's compromise of releasing a limited number of stamps— not through post offices, but through mail order fulfillment—is a decision I can reluctantly accept.

I appreciate your firm commitment to destroy the remainder of the incorrect sheets and look forward to joining you at the dedication ceremony of the new Legends of the West stamp later this year.

> Sincerely,
> Frank Phillips, Jr.

On June 9, the United States Postal Service issued a news release stating:

> The U.S. Postal Service will sell 150,000 sheets of Legends of the West stamps containing an incorrect portrait of cowboy Bill Pickett, Chairman of the Postal Board of Governors, announced today.
> The Postal Service had earlier announced it would destroy all 250 million stamps, including 5.2 million sheets that had been distributed and recalled after members of the Pickett family said the image on the Bill Pickett stamp was actually his brother Ben Pickett. "The inadvertent sale of 183 sheets of the Legends stamps created an unintended rarity in the market-place, making it expensive for collectors to maintain a complete stamp collection," Winters said. "The sale of 150,000 sheets of the recalled stamps gives everyone a chance to own a collectible."

The sale of the 183 erroneous sheets led to thousands of letters from collectors, dealers, and cover manufacturers asking the postal service to reconsider its decision to destroy the stamps. Editorials in the philatelic press also strongly urged the postal service not to withhold the stamps after the sales of the sheets became known.

Winters agreed, noting that the Postal Service wished "to balance the interests of the philatelic community with its respect for the interests of the Pickett family."

After consulting the Pickett family, the decision was made to sell one hundred fifty thousand sheets of the original "Legends" stamps and to destroy the remainder, Winters said. "The decision was based on two factors. One, it will alleviate collectors' concerns about the unintended rarity. Two, if sold out, the Postal Service will recover the cost of the original printing of the stamps," he added.

The press release continued:

In order to make the sheets available to the maximum number of individuals, sale of the recalled stamps will be limited to one order per customer, one sheet per order. Each sheet will be shipped by priority mail in protective plastic sleeves. The stamps will be sold by mail order only, with fulfillment beginning Dec. 1, 1994. No telephone orders will be accepted. In order to give all customers an equal opportunity to purchase the stamps, only orders postmarked between Oct. 1 and Oct. 31 will be accepted and will be filled based on the date of postmark. Those interested in obtaining a sheet of the recalled stamps should send a check, domestic money order or international money order drawn on an American bank for $8.70 (the $5.80 face value of the stamps plus a $2.90 shipping and handling) . . .

The release went on to give the mailing address and to state that major credit card payment would be accepted. It continued:

The Postal Service also announced that it is proceeding with printing of revised sheets of the Legends stamps, having completed an extensive review of the subjects. The review came after the Pickett discovery, which also prompted others interested in the stamps to raise creative differences. Only the Bill Pickett image and his date of birth will be changed when the revised Legends stamps are released this year.

That deal, however, was not good enough for many of the collectors. They contended that the compromise would not prevent the creation of a rarity because the one hundred fifty thousand uncorrected panes would be quickly gobbled up, and their value would increase. Although the price would not go as high as it would without the compromise, it would go high enough to prevent some stamp enthusiasts from completing their collections. There was widespread speculation that the one hundred fifty thousand Ben Pickett stamps would be sold out on the first day they were made available.

On June 30, Unicover, a Cheyenne, Wyoming, company that produces first-day covers and various stamp-related products and serves as a representative for various foreign postal administrations, filed a lawsuit to prevent the execution of the compromise plan. In that lawsuit, Unicover sought preliminary and permanent injunctions to prevent the Pickett error stamps from being destroyed and asked that all 5.2 million of the Legends panes be put on sale.

Only by doing so, Unicover argued, could the creation of a philatelic rarity be avoided, and it accused the postal service of violating its own regulations in planning to destroy most of the stamps. It insisted the one hundred fifty thousand stamps that would be issued under the Postal Service would meet the needs of less than three out of a hundred serious collectors. That calculation, it said, did not take into consideration members of the public who would be interested in obtaining one of the panes because of all the publicity that resulted from the error on the Pickett stamp. Although the proposed compromise had caused some of the astronomical figures on the price of the stamp to evaporate, Unicover still maintained the one hundred fifty thousand erroneous panes could be worth $100 to $350 each.

On July 1, U.S. District Judge Alan B. Johnson issued a temporary restraining order preventing the postal service from destroying any of the recalled stamps for twenty days. On July 15, Mystic Stamp Co. Of Camden, New York, joined Unicover as an intervenor in the lawsuit making essentially the same arguments. The lawsuits proved futile. When the period of the temporary restraining order ended, the court approved the postal service plan. Judge Johnson maintained that the "integrity" of the United States stamp program was at stake, and the postal service should not be required to distribute stamps with incorrect images on them.

In early October, collectors were to be allowed to send in their orders for the uncorrected stamps. In December, those who got their orders in before the supply ran out were to receive their stamps. Simultaneously, the new "Legends of the West" panes with the real Bill Pickett were to go on sale.

The great stamp snafu worked in Bill Pickett's favor. It generated more publicity and enhanced his reputation like nothing else since his life-and-death struggle in the bullring in Mexico City, and he was definitely hotter than Elvis in stamp collecting circles.

....

Chapter Seventeen

The Legacy

HEN HE WAS LITERALLY PICKING UP NICKELS and dimes for his performances, Bill Pickett could not in his wildest visions have foreseen the day when a bulldogger named Steve Duhon would rake in $113,450 in prize money in one year and win $63,611 of that in one week. Duhon, a thirty-one-year-old professional rodeo cowboy from Opelousas, Louisiana, hauled down his third world steer wrestling championship in 1993, wrapping up the title with a spectacular performance at the National Finals Rodeo. In that week-long competition, Duhon dropped ten steers in 49.3 seconds. In 1986, when he won his first championship, he polished off a steer in three seconds flat, which was a record for the National Finals competition.

Duhon, who won back-to-back titles in 1986 and 1987, sat out the 1991 and 1992 rodeo seasons because his father was seriously ill. He finished third in the world championship competition in 1992. Four-time world steer wrestling champion John W. Jones, Jr. of Morro Bay, California, had predicted that Duhon would win the title in 1993, and Duhon said, after doing so, that he was Jones's biggest fan and that Jones was "the greatest bulldogger who ever walked the face of the earth." A lot of old-timers might take issue with that. They would insist that the greatest bulldogger ever was the man who invented the sport, Bill Pickett. Duhon, of course, wasn't thinking back that far. He meant no historical slight. His frame of reference was people he'd actually seen jump on a steer and throw it down. And he was referring to the sport of steer wrestling the way it is officially done today.

By the standards of today's steer wrestling, Pickett's times would not have earned him many purses. But for most of his career, Pickett was not competing. He didn't start that until he was well advanced in years. It was out of his peerless exhibitions of skill, strength, and guts that the modern sport of steer wrestling, which has become so lucrative for the likes of Duhon, evolved. As has been pointed out previously, Pickett and his contemporaries bulldogged much larger animals, averaging 800 to 1,000 pounds, while the steers being dogged today are more in the 400- to 500-pound range. There is quite a difference between a 145-pound man like Pickett dogging a 1000-pound steer and a 240-pound man like Duhon wrestling down a 500-pound animal. That comparison is by no means intended to disparage modern steer wrestling or Duhon, who is a fantastic athlete. Steer wrestling is a thrilling and dangerous sport with a perilous beauty that makes it indispensable to rodeo. Nevertheless, any suggestion that anyone is or was a greater bulldogger than the guy who invented the sport needs to be put in proper perspective.

(See Appendix B: Hinkle's List of the Best Bulldoggers)

Back in 1967, Milt Hinkle put together a list of bulldog-gers he considered to be some of the best who ever lived. Many of those on Hinkle's list had stopped competing before the Pro Rodeo Cowboys Association's official listing of champions commenced in 1929. Only four of those official world champions are on Hinkle's list, which may say some-thing or nothing at all. It could be that those four are the only official champions Hinkle ever saw perform. Nevertheless, it is puzzling that Hinkle did not take note of Homer Pettigrew of Grady, New Mexico, who dominated the sport in the 1940s, winning the championship in 1940, 1942, 1943, 1944, 1945, and 1948.

(See Appendix C: The P.R.C.A.'s Roster of Champions)

Duhon, Jones, and Ote Berry, the 1992 champion, who also is a three-time champion, seemingly would have to surpass Pettigrew's seven world championships to be considered the greatest modern bulldogger. Pickett, of course, has the all-time distinction wrapped up without ever having won a champi-onship. All of them, of course, have far exceeded Pettigrew's prize money. In 1949, when he won his last world champi-onship, Pettigrew only banked $9,906 in prize money.

In 1991, Berry pocketed $116,674 in prize money, with $54,539 of that won at the finals. Added to the prize money, however, is income from product and services endorsements and such valuable prizes as the pickup truck Duhon received in addition to his prize money for winning the Dodge Truck Series Championship.

The top fifteen bulldoggers in the world won a total of $1,041,780 prize money in 1993. Again, that doesn't count endorsements and other incentives. Moreover, those fifteen represent only the tip of the iceberg of the phenomenon Bill Pickett started. Steer wrestling is a featured event in most of the hundreds of rodeos that take place every year in the United States and Canada. The top fifteen steer wrestlers get invited to the National Finals Rodeo for accumulating the most points and prize money from various P.R.C.A. approved events. To be in the running, a steer wrestler has to participate almost full-time in the activity. Scores do so. Hundreds more are part-time bulldoggers who make a few local or circuit competitions. All of that adds up to a lot of prize money. But it also means big bills for equipment, travel, and animal care. Without those incentives, even the top cowboys' earnings could be gobbled up by maintenance costs.

At the same time, steer wrestling is an essential part of the rodeo culture that generates millions of dollars in sales of western clothing, leather crafts, trucks, horse trailers, livestock food, human beverages, and western-style entertainment.

This megabucks bonanza derives in large measure from the risky antics of an old-time cowboy who earned twelve bucks a week.

As of the middle of 1994, no black cowboy had succeeded in making it into the top fifteen steer wrestlers invited to the National Finals. There were a number of them involved at the circuit level. But rodeo is an expensive avocation, and most black cowboys can only afford to participate in it on a part-time basis. Few black bulldoggers have attracted much notice through the years. One of them who was frequently named was Joe Pickett. Some authors have referred to him as Bill Pickett's nephew, but he was not related to the original bulldogger at all. However, Willie Wilson of Ardmore, Oklahoma, one of Bill Pickett's great-grandsons, did do a lot of bulldogging in the 1970s.

Inasmuch as Bill Pickett was an all-around cowboy, black cowboys, regardless of their specialties, hold him in high regard. They owe him as much as the steer wrestlers because of their ethnic linkage. As of the middle of 1994, only two black cowboys had won world championship buckles. The first to do so was Charles Sampson, who won the bull-riding championship in 1982, accumulating record-setting prize money in the event that year of $91,402. Sampson was twenty-four years old at the time. The diminutive (five feet, four inches; 133 pounds) Sampson came from an unlikely background for a rodeo champion. A native of Los Angeles, he personifies the concept of the urban cowboy. His interest in rodeo was sparked when, at the age of ten, he paid a quarter to ride a pony around a ring five times at a neighborhood circus.

Bitten by the riding bug, Sampson collected empty bottles on his way to school and sold them to a liquor store to pay for more rides. At the age of eleven he got a job at a stable where he met several black cowboys who fascinated him with stories about rodeo and taught him some of the skills. He began practicing roping on pets and other children. There were thirteen kids in his family.

One of the black cowboys who had a strong influence on Sampson was the veteran bull rider Myrtis Dightman, who made the national finals several times. In 1966, Dightman, of Houston, Texas, finished ninth, with overall winnings of $9,154; in 1967, he was third with $16,014; in 1968, he was third again with $15,348; in 1969, he was fifteenth with $10,331; and in 1970, he was thirteenth with $12,134.

Dightman steered Sampson toward bull riding, and by the age of thirteen, the 106-pounder already had ridden his first bull. After competing in amateur rodeos, Sampson won a rodeo scholarship to Central Arizona College in Coolidge. He left college before graduating to turn professional, which meant riding about thirty bulls a month in rodeos that were mostly in the South and Southwest. It was a life of hard work and pain. Sampson suffered as many injuries as the legendary Pickett, including three leg fractures, knee damage, a split sternum, broken fingers, several concussions, and a punctured lung.

A few months after winning the bull riding world championship, Sampson was giving a command performance for President Ronald Reagan, members of Congress, and hundreds of other dignitaries at Landover, Maryland, when he suffered some of his most serious injuries. He was aboard a bull named Kiss Me. The bull came out bucking furiously. It reared its head up just as Sampson's was coming down. The head butt did no damage to Kiss Me, but it left Sampson with a cracked forehead, a broken jaw, and a broken chin. Kiss Me's head smashed Sampson's chances of repeating as a national champion. His injuries forced him to sit out the 1983 national finals in Oklahoma City. He still finished sixth in the world in 1983 with winnings of $54,000. In 1984, he came back to $65,815 and placed second in the world to Don Gay of Mesquite, Texas. In 1985, he was fourth with $68,366; and in 1986, he was sixth with $89,272.

By the end of 1986, after eight years as a P.R.C.A. professional, Sampson had won more than a half-million dollars in official prize money, and he was far from being finished. He retired—make that semiretired—at the end of the 1993 season, after making it to the national finals ten times. He finished in ninth place in 1990 with winnings of $51,122. Sampson was joined in the finals that year by black bull rider Ervin Williams of Cheyenne, Wyoming, who finished in a tie for fourth place with three other riders. The twenty-seven-year-old Williams also made the national finals the following year, finishing ninth with winnings of $65,117.

Once when asked about the extent of racial discrimination in professional rodeo, Sampson gave an answer that called to mind Bill Pickett's way of saying much with few words:

> "I think how you make it, whether you are black or white or yellow, depends on your talent and drive. In modern rodeo, being white won't help you if you can't ride and being black won't hurt you if you can."

In his sophomore year as a fully qualified P.R.C.A. competitor Fred Whitfield of Cypress, Texas, tied ten calves faster than anyone had ever done before and won the Gold Buckle that identified him as the World's Champion Calf Roper of 1991. At the National Finals Rodeo in Las Vegas, Whitfield tied his ten calves in an unprecedented 91.7 seconds, eclipsing the old world mark of 102.6 seconds and shattering the national finals average of 10.9 seconds per calf. His highest time was 11 seconds, but he also had times of 8.3 seconds and 8.4 seconds. He brought the house to its feet for a thundering ovation when he secured his eighth calf in a lightning-quick 7.8 seconds.

In the process of becoming the first black cowboy to win the world calf roping title, Whitfield increased his prize money for the year to $70,609, which was $17,720 more than any calf roper had ever won before.

A year earlier, Whitfield had won the coveted title of Resistol Rookie of the Year with total winnings of $58,765. His biggest thrill that year, prior to the national finals came when he won the calf-roping event at the Cheyenne Frontier Days. His biggest single payday of 1990 came at the national finals, where he won $15,330. At that event, he received his Rookie of the Year buckle from country and western singer George Strait.

Whitfield's winning ways continued with some variation due to injuries, and by the middle of 1994, he was the hottest calf roper in the business. He once attributed much of his success to his horse, Ernie. He displayed an affection for the horse, similar to that of Bill Pickett toward Spradley, when he won the world title in 1991. He asked reporters and photographers to hold off a while until he could see about Ernie.

"I need to make sure he's taken care of. He's my livelihood," said Whitfield.

Bill Pickett's legacy to the sport of steer wrestling and to black cowboys is inestimable. The ethnic part of that legacy has received greater recognition in recent years, as increasingly African Americans have become interested in rodeo both as participants and spectators. The percentage of black P.R.C.A. cowboys remains relatively small largely because of the expense and the sacrifice involved. Nevertheless, a fascination with cowboy culture was growing among blacks in the nineties. Part of that had to do with changing portrayals of blacks in western movies and television shows and a new emphasis on multiculturalism in the study of American history in the schools. As more African Americans became aware of the roles their forebears played in the conquest and settlement of the American West, they began to relate more to that part of the American heritage and to the image of the cowboy in particular.

That reassessment of the significance of the cowboy can be summed up in two words: Bill Pickett. Whether or not they know anything about Pickett's life, most African Americans are familiar with the name. And when they say it or hear it, it means to them: "Yes, we were there, too."

There are, however, less generalized legacies. The historical attachment Taylor, Texas, has made to Bill Pickett stands out among them. In a belated commentary on Pickett's induction in the National Cowboy Hall of Fame in 1971, the *Taylor Daily Press* emphasized that "three Taylorites," Ray Condra, Ivan West, and Joe Casey were present at the posthumous awards ceremony. That article also stated that Pickett "lived in Taylor for a time, residing at 811 E. Second St., where a niece, Willie B. Royal, named for the famous cowboy, still resides, although not in the same house as her famous uncle."

In June 1983, Taylor High School transformed its library into an exhibition hall for two weeks for a display of painting, photographs, books, and memorabilia featuring Bill Pickett and included material on other Texas and local blacks of historical significance. That exhibition was brought to Taylor by the Adept New America Folk Center Program in Houston, Texas.

In February 1986, Taylor High School devoted its entire Black History Month observance to Pickett. That was the year Mrs. Royal was named chairman of Taylor's Bill Pickett Preservation Society. T-shirts were sold with Pickett's picture emblazoned on them to help support the society.

In May 1992, a Texas historical marker honoring Pickett was unveiled in Taylor's Heritage Square. A month later Taylor held its first annual "Bill Pickett Parade and Trail Ride," complete with catering. The parade kicked off at 10:00 A.M. and the trail ride to Noack, seven miles away, commenced at 1:30 P.M. The trek was made to Noack because legend has it that Pickett invented his bite 'em technique of bulldogging there. At 8:00 P.M. the Bill Pickett Rodeo was held in the Taylor Rodeo Arena.

Other cities, such as Ponca City, Marland, and Fort Worth, have forged similar historical linkages to Pickett, but none stronger than those of his hometown of Taylor, Texas.

Epilogue

....

❦

I began this story with Zack Miller's poem about Bill
Pickett. I think it fitting that I end it with one of my own
about Pickett. I wrote this in 1983, when Ron Tyler of the
Amon Carter Museum of Western Art in Fort Worth gave
me access to the museum's archives to peruse 1908 newspaper articles from Mexico City, containing accounts of Bill
Pickett's battle with Frijoli Chiquita.

BILL PICKETT AND LITTLE BEANS
by Cecil Johnson

He chose to wear his crimson shirt
Though bulls they say see red,
And blood is also of that hue
When on the sand it's shed.
Bill Pickett's blood they hoped would flow,
That crowd that wished him dead.

He rode into that angry place
His hat cocked to the right,
Mounted on a chestnut steed
Swift Spradley his delight,
And out to greet them charged the bull
Bill Pickett came to fight.

Not fight him like a matador
With blood red cape and sword,
But dog him like a longhorned steer
Or at least stay aboard
The beast for five minutes
Without his getting gored.

It was a contest made in Hell,
Blood thirst would drink its fill,
They knew no cowboy from the north
Possessed the guts or skill
To dominate a fighting bull
That had been bred to kill.

Into that ring of looming death
Came bull and man and horse,
The bet was set, the clock was wound
No time left for discourse,
Just man and beasts and bloody fate,
Too late to show remorse.

The crowd was screaming for his death,
They raised their voices high,
For he had mocked the thing they loved,
And so he had to die.

For all people have a thing they love,
A thing with which their pride
Their sense of being who they are
Is much identified;
Bullfighting was that thing for them
Who in that bullring cried:

"No man can hold a brave bull's horns,
No fool for gold and glory
Could jump onto a brave bull's hump
And live to tell the story."

The bull rushed forth with lowered head
Took aim at Spradley's rear
But the little horse stepped to the side
Just as the horns came near,
So close and yet not close enough
For Pickett to adhere.

Three times the raging Little Beans
(That was the name they cried)
Lunged at horse and rider;

Each time he was denied,
But Pickett could not climb aboard
The spotted killer's hide.

The cowboy had to make a choice,
And yet no choice had he,
To get upon the Little Beans
He had to let Spradley
Be savaged by the cruel horns;
Another way he couldn't see.

He had to watch a thing he loved
Endure that awful fate,
To grace that altar with his blood,
A sacrifice to hate.

With fierce resolve the killer bull
Gathered speed and vaulted;
Spradley tried to move away,
But Pickett held him halted
In the path of the bull's wrath,
Then Pickett somersaulted.

Upon the hump with his strong hands
Those gore-smeared horns he squeezed,
Those needle-sharp and slippery horns
His Spradley's blood had greased;

He held on as the big bull ran
And took him where it pleased.

It took him left, it took him right,
It slammed him on the walls;
It took him east, it took him west,
As if it heard the bawls
Of the crowd in the arena
With its "Death to Pickett" calls.

For he had mocked the thing they loved,
Or so they'd heard it said;
He'd thumbed his nose at their great sport,
And so they wished him dead.

"No man can grab a brave, brave bull
For gold and for his glory;
No fool can ride a fighting bull
And live to tell the story."

Around and around ran bull and man,
The cowboy held on fast,
And when the bull came to a stop
The arena was aghast;
Pickett jumped between the horns
And squeezed that neck so vast.

The cowboy squeezed with all his strength
To take the breath away.
He pressed his knees against the nose,
The bull began to sway,
He rocked him left, he rocked him right,
He thought he'd won the day.

That Little Beans so brave and mean
Stood statue still and muzzled,
While in the stands the Mexicans
Looked at each other puzzled;
No man could hold a killer bull . . .
They were totally bumfuzzled.

No man could choke a brave bull down
For money or for glory,
No man could mock their bullfighting
And live to tell the story.

It wasn't Pickett who had bet or scoffed at bullfighting.
His boss, of course, had done all that,
But it was Pickett in the ring,
And it was for Bill Pickett's death the crowd did sing.

The Dusky Demon held his pose
Waiting for the clock;
Then someone in that angry mob

Threw and hit him with a rock.
Other things came flying
Pelting, pounding man and bull,
Then came that awful shock.

The beer bottle that broke his ribs
Made Pickett lose his grip,
And that was all the bull needed
To start another trip
Around the sundrenched bullring
At a much faster clip.

The crowd was yelling for him
To shake Bill off and gore him
To lift him up and toss him high
And let his blood and entrails fly,
For he had mocked the thing they love,
And so he had to die.

Although Bill Pickett lost his hold,
He did not die that day;
Cowboys came and matadors
And helped him get away;

His little horse named Spradley
Survived his goring in the fray.

One man did hold a brave bull's horns
And earned a share of glory.
Bill Pickett rode a killer bull
And lived to tell the story.

....

Pickett's Peers:
Nat Love to Lonesome Dove

S THE GENERAL PUBLIC'S KNOWLEDGE OF black cowboys goes, Bill Pickett's name comes closer to being a household word than that of any other African American who ever rode across the pages of the history of the American West. That's understandable because Pickett was in show business, and for a time his fame was roughly equivalent to that of such contemporary professional athletes as Michael Jordan. Moreover, there has been frequent dropping of Pickett's name in recent years in movies and television public affairs programs when mention is made of blacks in connection with things western. During the summer of 1994, an old-fashioned Wild West show was staged on weekends in the Cowtown Coliseum in Fort Worth, Texas's historic Stockyards tourist center. The featured attraction of that so-called "Pawnee Bill's Wild West Show" was a cowboy named Timmy Brooks, who portrayed Bill Pickett and bulldogged steers bite 'em style.

Nevertheless, Pickett was not an isolated phenomenon. There were others who left indelible marks on the culture and heritage of the American West. Some of them, like Nat Love, were as fascinating in their own ways as Pickett. Love has been referred to previously as a braggart. And he was very prone to exaggeration and self-promotion. In that respect, he was a kind of black Buffalo Bill. E. E. Cummings might just as easily have written his famous Buffalo Bill poem about Love, who claimed in his autobiography to be the legendary gunfighter "Deadwood Dick" of Deadwood, South Dakota. Cummings could have written: "Deadwood Dick's defunct . . . who used to ride the range from Dakota to Arizona . . .and shoot down one, two, three, four, five bandits and Indians just like that . . . Jesus, he was a daring man . . . and what I want to know is . . . how do you like your brownskinned boy, Mr. Death?"

Love was not the "Deadwood Dick," who was supposed to be the fastest and straightest shooting gunfighter in that wild and woolly South Dakota town where Wild Bill Hickok was gunned down. As a matter of fact, there probably was no such person, although scores of cowboys staked claim to being that shadowy figure. Love based his claim to that title because in dime novels Deadwood Dick was also known as the "Black Rider of the Black Hills." Still, Love had a legitimate claim to the nickname Deadwood Dick, but he earned that distinction in another Deadwood.

Nat Love was actually a fast-learning easterner. Born in Ohio, he went west as a young man to Dodge City, Kansas, where he demonstrated enough horsemanship to land a job with the Duval Ranch. During his three-year hitch with that outfit, Love picked up the nickname "Red River Dick." While there Love, according to his account, had several skirmishes with Indians and was once taken prisoner by Chief Yellow Dog's band of black and Indian half-breeds.

In 1872, Red River Dick hired on with the Gallanger Company, whose ranch sprawled for miles along the Gila River in southern Arizona. Love had a gift for languages, and he picked up Spanish quickly, enabling him to interact effectively with Mexicans on both sides of the border. He became such a valued hand that he was elevated to brand reader. At all roundups he was given responsibility for picking out all the cattle belonging to the home ranch, detecting brands that had been modified and generally overseeing all of the branding.

It was in 1876 at a Fourth of July roping contest in Deadwood, Arizona, that Red River Dick actually picked up the monicker Deadwood Dick. He was a member of a crew that had delivered three thousand head of cattle to that town. There had been a recent discovery of gold in the area by the Homestead Mines. The town was overflowing with miners, cowboys, and gunslingers. A prize of two hundred dollars was offered by a group of miners and gamblers to the cowboy who could rope, saddle, and ride a mustang in the shortest span of time. Love completed the task in nine minutes. No other cowboy came close. Love also hit the bull's eye with all fourteen of his rifle shots and ten of twelve pistol shots to take the marksmanship prize.

Deadwood Dick claimed to have been an acquaintance of Billy the Kid and to have been at the Maxwell Ranch when the Kid was killed. But Love gave up his wild cowboy ways in 1889, when he got married. He settled down and took a job as a Pullman porter on the Denver and Rio Grande Railroad and wrote of his adventures.

Matthew "Bones" Hooks also spent his last working years as a Pullman porter. One of the last cowboys to trail herds up the Chisholm Trail from Texas to Dodge City, Hooks was known as one of the greatest bronc busters who ever lived. His most famous feat of that kind actually came after he had left the range and taken to the trains. That happened when he was pitted against a horse that was supposed to be unridable. Every cowboy who had mounted the so-called "Hurricane Deck" had come away bruised, battered, and defeated. Hooks accepted the challenge to ride the "ton of dynamite," and the event attracted spectators from throughout West Texas. Hooks was working at the time for the Santa Fe Railroad, and when his train pulled into the station at Pampa, Texas, the Hurricane Deck was there saddled and ready for him.

Hooks led the stormy beast into an open field, mounted it without any help, and stuck in the saddle like glue until the hurricane abated. With the Hurricane Deck subdued and ready to make someone a good saddle horse, Hooks reboarded the train right on schedule and completed his run.

As much as for his horsemanship, Hooks, who made his home in Abilene, Texas, until he died in 1951, acquired considerable notice for his homespun philosophizing. A thinking man's cowboy, Hooks placed great emphasis on the role of women and the importance of the family in bringing order, stability, and prosperity to the western frontier. He took it upon himself to pay tribute to the great cowboys and other distinguished persons who made important contributions to the development of the American West. His tributes took the form of bouquets of white flowers, which he called "White Guerdons of Honor." The first of those white guerdons was sent to a friend with whom he rode the range for many years named Tom Clayton, who was dying from injuries suffered in a fall from his horse. Clayton's mother placed the white flowers on his grave when he died. A few of those guerdons went to black cowboys whose names ring no historically significant bells. Among them were: Bill Freeman of the "Quarter Circle Heart," Dan Sowell of the "Figure 4," and Brook Lee of "Diamond Trail."

Hooks also sent white guerdons in his latter years to distinguished persons who had no ostensible connection to the heritage of the American West. Included among them were Franklin and Eleanor Roosevelt, Winston Churchill, and heavyweight boxing champion Joe Louis.

Unlike Love and Hooks, "Eighty" John Wallace, seeing the sun setting on the days of the open range, did not take to the rails. He showed foresight and enterprise and took cowpunching to its next evolutionary step.

"Eighty" John got his numerical first nickname from his long association with cattleman Clay Mann, all of whose cattle were branded on both sides with the huge, untamperable number eight-zero. Born in Victoria County, Texas, ten years before Bill Pickett, Wallace grew up learning all about cattle. He had already made his first trail drive through Indian country. At eighteen, he hooked up with John Nunn's UWN outfit that had eight thousand cattle on the range. After working for Nunn for a year and a half, Wallace signed on with Clay Mann and stayed with his ranch for the next fourteen years, learning every aspect of the cattle business and serving as Mann's banker.

Wallace possessed a phenomenal ability to estimate the number of cattle in a herd. Mann once won a sizable bet by relying on Wallace's extraordinary computational faculty. Several cattlemen were speculating on the size of a large herd, and the built-up pot that was to go to the one whose estimate came closest. Mann had Wallace take a quick gander at the herd before putting up his money. Wallace told him there were five thousand head in the herd. The actual number turned out to be 4,975.

After also working for such cattle barons as the Elwoods of Spade Ranch, Winfield Scott, Gus O'Keefe, and Sug Robertson, Wallace saw that the days of the open range and free grass were coming to an end, and so were a lot of jobs for cowhands. He bought land with his savings over the years out of his $30-a-month wages and fenced it. When the depression hit in 1929, Wallace was able to weather it. The twelve hundred acres he owned in Mitchell County were debt clear. Even his taxes were paid up completely. For three decades Wallace was a member of the Texas and Southwest Cattle Raisers Association and a financial adviser to many of his white and black neighbors.

Bob Leavit was another black cowboy with an entrepreneurial penchant. His enterprise, however, tended in another direction from Wallace's. Leavit worked for the huge XIT Ranch in Texas and was one of the members of the first crews to drive a herd up from Texas to XIT's two-million acre spread in Montana. Instead of returning to Texas with the rest of the crew, after the cattle had been delivered, Leavit decided to stay on in Montana. He was an excellent all-around cowhand, but he saw no future in that line of work. He hankered for an easier life with more financial rewards.

Leavit saved up his pay and used it to build a saloon in Miles City, Montana. The saloon became a kind of Mecca for cowboys on ranches in the region, as well as those driving herds up from the Southwest. The cowboys flocked to Leavit's saloon to drink, gamble, and spin tall yarns about life on the range and the action in the cow towns along the cattle trails. Leavit was generous with credit but tough on deadbeats. When a cowboy wouldn't pay, Leavit would give him another free drink. What he put in that free drink no one ever knew, but it would set a cowboys throat and insides on fire and send him flying out of Bob Leavit's saloon gasping for air.

Some noteworthy black cowboys, as previously noted, were remembered only by their first names and some adjective, either complimentary or pejorative. One cowboy known simply as "Broncho" Sam was one of the best bronc busters on the range, but he earned a dubious place in history by virtue of his penchant for rowdy fun. When the crew Sam had come up the rail with to Cheyenne decided to have some extra fun, they picked Sam to provide it. Their idea was to have some cowboy ride the biggest longhorn in the herd down Cheyenne's Main Street. They picked Sam because he was the best rider in the bunch, and Sam liked the idea. They saddled up the longhorn, and Sam climbed upon it. They yelled and created such a ruckus that the wild steer panicked. The animal bawled, pitched, and bucked frantically, but Sam held on. Suddenly, the animal ceased its violent motions as he and Sam approached a clothing store. Seeing its reflection in the window of the store, the steer stood transfixed for a moment. Then it charged through the glass, carrying Sam with it. Glass splattered all over the boardwalk and inside the store, where clothes and other merchandise were scattered into a shambles. Then the steer charged back through the shattered window out into the street again and resumed trying to throw Sam off its back.

After roping the longhorn and taking it back to the herd, the sobered-up cowboys went back into town to face the music. They were met by a group of furious shopkeepers, but they calmed down when Sam calmly dished out $350 and settled their claims for damages.

Sam also was involved in a similar caper in Laramie, Wyoming. The ranch crew challenged him to ride his horse up the steps of Laramie's Frontier Hotel. He had almost made it to the top of the classy hotel's steep front steps when the stairway collapsed. Sam walked away again unhurt, except in his wallet.

The ordeal of black cowboy George Glenn may have provided part of the inspiration for one of the best-selling novels of recent years. Glenn was employed by R. B. Johnson on a ranch in Colorado County, Texas. Johnson led a crew on a drive up the Chisholm Trail to Abilene, Kansas. When they reached Abilene, Johnson suffered a fatal heart attack. The crew had him embalmed and buried him there. When the crew returned to Texas and told of the tragedy, Glenn said they should have brought him home because he knew Johnson wanted to be buried in the family cemetery there in Colorado County.

Glenn proposed that some of them go back up the trail, dig Johnson up, and bring him home to Texas. Everyone else, however, dismissed the idea as foolish sentimentality, and when Glenn said he'd do it alone if no one would go with him, they called him crazy. So Glenn hitched up a wagon and set out on that insane journey alone. He didn't even stay in Abilene a day to rest after finding the grave, digging up the body, and loading it into the wagon. After taking on a few supplies, he headed back down that lonesome trail he'd just come up. The journey up to Kansas had been bad enough. The trip back turned quickly into a nightmare.

The extra weight of the body in the coffin in the wagon caused more wear and tear on the wheels, and he had to make frequent repairs. Then the drenching rains came, turning the trails into muddy quagmires. It took back-wrenching exertions to continually pull and push the wagon out of holes and ruts. Several times, the wagon was almost swept away when he had to cross swollen streams.

He slept little for fear of hostile Indians or bandits. One man alone with a corpse didn't stand much of a chance in an ambush. Some of the people he did meet on the way either told him outright that he was insane or just treated him that way. The word had spread all along the trail that some black fool was carrying a corpse all the way from Kansas to Texas in a wagon.

Exposure and exhaustion finally took their toll, and Glenn came down with pneumonia. He lay there outdoors with a dead man, wheezing, coughing, and alternately burning up and freezing to death, and praying that someone would find both their bodies and take them back to Texas to be buried. But Glenn did not die. He recovered his strength, completed his journey, and buried Johnson in the family cemetery. The dangerous and exhausting trip had taken forty-two days.

It is conceivable that novelist Larry McMurtry had never heard George Glenn's extraordinary exhibition of courage, strength, dogged determination, and loyalty when he wrote *Lonesome Dove*. It is possible that the remarkable section of the novel in which Captain Call transports Gus's body back home to *Lonesome Dove* was purely a figment of McMurtry's rich imagination. That is unlikely, however, because McMurtry is well-versed in the lore of the American West, particularly the

Texas part of it. It is no crime, however, if he did fictionalize Glenn's story for his purposes. It's a good yarn. Whether or not McMurtry had heard of Glenn's exploit, his fictional account of Captain Call taking Gus home amounts to a great tribute to an obscure black cowboy who actually did it.

Glenn's exploit called to mind Bill Pickett's plea to Joe Miller to take him back to Oklahoma to be buried should he have been killed by the killer bull in Mexico City.

....

Hinkle's List of the Best Bulldoggers

❦

Hinkle's list of best bulldoggers included: Harold Cox, J. O. Banks, Mike Hastings, Dutch Sidell, Ken Maynard, Scout Maish, Hershell Ross, Harry Hazleton, Skeeter Bill Robbins, Wild Jim Lynch, Delbert Bledso, Lee Robinson, Slim Cassidy, Frank McCarroll, George (Fig) Newton, George Pittman, Jerry Wright, J. M. Smith, Esteven Clemento, Curley Griffin, Bert Weams, Booger Red, Jr., Angelo Hughes, Buddy McDuff, Ben Johnson, Sr., John McIntire, Jack (Fingers) Armstrong, Frank Brion, Slim Allen, Ed Herrin, Fred Alvord, Bob Belcher, Red Thompson, Hug Bennett, Everett Bowman, John Bowman, Buff Brady, Sr., Louis Brooks, Bill Brown, Eddie Cameron, John Henry, Tom Henderson, Dutch Hyler, Red Remington, Tom Hogan, Jack Jackson, Slats Jacobs, Buck Jones, John Jordan, Herman Linder, Andy Curtis, Ed Davis, Buddie McDuff, Orvall Sumwall, Homer Todd, Andy Robinson, Johnny Jud, Hank Keenan, Billy Keen, Ken Bowen,

Buck Lucas, Howard McCory, Mickey McCory, Rusty McGinty, Shorty McCory, Bill Macken, Joe Blackstone, Vick Blackstone, Chip Morris, Don Nesbitt, Jim Nesbitt, Dan Offitt, Cliff King, Tex Parker, Peavine Slim Cy Perkins, Slim Gamble, Roy Quick, Slim Riley, Gene Ross, Paddy Ryan, Lloyd Saunders, Floyd Stillings, Cheyenne Kiser, Paul Hansen, Earl Thode, Shorty Porter, Shorty Creed, Charlie (Chick) Johnson, Roy Correll, Bill Sawyers, John Creather, Bob Crosby, Lynn Huskey, Speedy Densmore, Jack Fritz, Frank Gable, Tex Smith, Roy Gafford, Pinkey Gist, Tuck Greenough, Frank Butler, Shorty Grugan, Jay Snively, Red Hammerschardt, George Hinkle, Chick Hannon, Jim Wilke, Shorty Richer, Rube Roberts, Dallas Conely, Ed Davis, Dude Smith, Grady Smith, Leonard Stroud, Fritz Truan, Dick Truitt, Leonard Ward, Hub Whiteman, Dave Whyte, Len Wier, Soapy Williams, Olie Rice, and George Yareley.

Appendix C

....

The P.R.C.A.'s Roster of
Champions

❦

The P.R.C.A.'s roster of champions includes: Gene Ross, Sayre, Oklahoma, 1929; Everett Bowman, Hillside, Arizona, 1930; Gene Ross, 1931; Hugh Bennett, Fort Thomas, Arizona, 1932; Everett Bowman, Hillside, Arizona, 1933; Shorty Ricker, Ranger, Texas, 1934; Everett Bowman, 1935; Jack Kershner, Miles City, Montana, 1936; Ross, 1937; Bowman, 1938; Harry Hart, Pocatello, Idaho, 1939; Homer Pettigrew, Grady, New Mexico, 1940; Hub Whiteman, Clarksville, Texas, 1941; Pettigrew, 1942; Pettigrew, 1943; Pettigrew, 1944; Pettigrew, 1945; Dave Campbell, Las Vegas, Nevada, 1946; Todd Whatley, Hugo, Oklahoma, 1947; Pettigrew, 1948; Bill McGuire, Fort Worth, Texas, 1949; Bill Linderman, Red Lodge, Montana, 1950; Dub Phillips, San Angelo, Texas, 1951; Harley May, Oakdale, California, 1952; Ross Dollarhide, Lakeview, Oregon, 1953; James Bynum, Forreston, Texas, 1954; Benny Combs, Checotah, Oklahoma,

1955; Harley May, Oakdale, California, 1956; Willard Combs, Checotah, Oklahoma, 1957; James Bynum, Forreston, Texas, 1958; Harry Charters, Melba, Idaho, 1959; Bob A. Robinson, Rockland, Idaho, 1960; Bynum, Forreston, Texas, 1961; Tom Nesmith, Bethel, Oklahoma, 1962; Bynum, 1963; C. R. Boucher, Burkburnett, Texas, 1964: May, 1965; Jack Roddy, San Jose, California, 1966; Roy Duval, Boynton, Oklahoma, 1967; Roddy, 1968; Duval, 1969; John W. Jones, Morro Bay, California, 1970; Billy Hale, Checotah, Oklahoma, 1971; Roy Duval, Warner, Oklahoma, 1972; Bob Marshall, San Martin, California, 1973; Tommy Puryear, Norman, Oklahoma, 1974; Frank Shepperson, Midwest, Wyoming, 1975; Rick Bradley, Burkburnett, Texas, 1976.; Tom Ferguson, Miami, Oklahoma, 1977; Ferguson, 1978; Stan Williamson, Kellyville, Oklahoma, 1979; Butch Myers, Welda, Kansas, 1980; Byron Walker, Ennis, Texas, 1981; Williamson, 1982; Joel Edmonson, Columbus, Kansas, 1983; Jones, 1984; Ote Berry, Gordon, Nebraska, 1985; Duhon, 1986; Duhon, 1987; Jones, 1988; Jones, 1989; Berry, 1990; Berry, 1991; Mark Roy, Dalemead, Alberta, Canada, 1992; Duhon, 1993.

Bibliography

❧

BOOKS

Branch, Hettye Wallace. *The Story of 80 John.* New York: Greenwich Book Publishers Inc., 1960.

Brown, William R. Imagemaker: *Will Rogers and the American Dream.* Columbia, Missouri: University of Missouri Press, 1970.

Clancy, Foghorn. *My 50 Years in Rodeo.* San Antonio, Texas: Naylor Co., 1952.

Collings, Ellsworth and Allma Miller England. *The 101 Ranch.* Norman, Oklahoma: University of Oklahoma Press, 1938.

Conrad, Barnaby. *La Fiesta Brava: The Art of the Bull Ring.* Boston: Houghton Mifflin Co., 1950.

Coolidge, Dane. *Texas Cowboys.* New York: E. P. Dutton and Co., 1937.

Day, Beth. *America's First Cowgirl, Lucille Mulhall.* New York: Julian Messner Co., 1955.

Dunham, Phillip and Everett L. Jones. *The Negro Cowboys*. New York: Dodd, Mead and Co., 1956.

Fredrickson, Kristine. *American Rodeo*. College Station, Texas: Texas A & M University Press, 1985.

Gibson, Fred. *Fabulous Empire*. Boston: Houghton Mifflin Co., 1946.

Hanes, Colonel Bailey. *Bill Pickett: Bulldogger*. Norman, Oklahoma: University of Oklahoma Press, 1977.

Katz, William L. *The Black West*. New York: Doubleday and Co., 1973.

Lamar, Howard R., ed. *Encyclopedia of the American West*. New York: Thomas Y. Crowell Co., 1977.

Le Compte, Mary Lou. *Cowgirls of the Rodeo*. Urbana, Illinois, and Chicago: University of Illinois, 1993.

O'Brien, Essie Forrester. *The First Bulldogger*. San Antonio, Texas: Naylor and Co., 1961.

O'Neal, Bill. *The Arizona Rangers*. Austin, Texas: Eakin Press, 1987.

Rainey, Buck. *Saddle Aces of the Cinema*. London: A. S. Bower and Co. Inc., 1980.

Russell, Don. *The Wild West*. Fort Worth: Amon Carter Museum of Western Art, 1970.

Savitt, Sam. *Rodeo Cowboys, Bulls, and Broncs*. New York: Garden City, 1963.

Shirley, Glenn. *Buckskin and Spurs*. New York: Hastings, 1958.

Slatta, Richard W. *Cowboys of the Americas*. New Haven, Connecticut, and London: Yale University Press, 1990.

Sutherland, Donald. *The Yellow Earl*. New York: Copyright Donald Sutherland, 1956.

Terry, Cleo and Ossie Wilson. *The Rawhide Tree*. Clarendon, Texas: Clarendon Press, 1957.

Westermeir, Clifford P. *Man, Beast and Dust*. Lincoln, Nebraska: University of Nebraska Press, 1947.

Weston, Jack L. *The Real American Cowboy*. New York: New Amsterdam Books, 1985.

Yost, Nellie Snyder. *Buffalo Bill*. Chicago: Swallow Press, 1979.

ARTICLES

Bloom, Sam. "Black Trailblazers and Cowboys," *Real West* (March 1965): 30-34.

Gill, Gale. "Texas Trail Ride, Negro Cowboys," *Ebony* (May 1963):115-126.

Harmon, John H. "Black Cowboys are Real," *Crisis* (September 1940): 280-284.

Hinkle, Milt. "A Texan Hits the Pampas," *Old West*, Vol. II, No. 1 (fall 1965):2-8; 40-44.

"Bulldoggers," *True West*, Vol. XV, No. 2 (November-December, 1967): 38-39.

"The Dusky Demon," *True West*, Vol. VIII, No. 6 (July-August, 1961): 31; 55-57.

— "Spradley of the 101," *True West*, Vol. XII, No. 1 (September-October, 1964): 24-25; 50.

Howe, J. D. "Cowboy Festival in Wyoming," *Harper's Weekly* (8 October 1904): 15; 40-41.

Katiagan, Madelon B. "The Fabulous 101," *True West*, Vol. VIII, No. 1 (September-October, 1960): 6-12; 50.

Lutz, Aleta. "The 101 Ranch and the Buffalo Bulldogger," *Oklahoma Today* (Summer 1962): 6-7.

Mundis, Jerrold J. "He Took the Bull by the Horns," *American Heritage*, Vol. XIX, No. 1 (December 1967): 50-55.

Porter, Willard H. "Pickett Really Started Something," *The Cattleman* (September 1953): 1058-1059.

Pro-Rodeo Sports News,

(year-end edition, 1989).

(year-end edition, 1990).

(year-end edition, 1991).

(year-end edition, 1993).

"Taking the Bull by the Horns Again," *Ebony* (March 1985): 146-149.

NEWSPAPERS

Arizona (Phoenix) *Republican*, 6 May 1905; 7 May 1905.

Fort Worth Telegram, 22 March 1905.

Fort Worth Star and Telegram, 4 January 1909, morning edition; 5 January 1909, evening edition.

Fort Worth Star-Telegram, 6 June 1985, morning edition ; 24 May 1987.

Linn's (Ohio) Stamp News, Sidney, Ohio, 24 January 1994; 14 February 1994; 21 February 1994; 28 February 1994; 7 March 1994; 4 April 1994; 25 April 1994; 2 May 1994; 4 July 1994; 18 July 1994; 1 August 1994.

London Times, London, England, 16 April 1932.

New York Times, New York City, 14 January 1994.

Taylor (Texas) *Daily Press*, Taylor, Texas, 13 June 1983; 13 February 1986; 26 May 1992.